A HISTORY OF
SINGAPORE
ARCHITECTURE

279 River Valley Road

A HISTORY OF SINGAPORE ARCHITECTURE

The Making of a City

JANE BEAMISH &
JANE FERGUSON

GRAHAM BRASH

Errata

p.157.   *The Singapore Conference Hall was by*
         Malayan Architects Co-Partnership

p.169–170.   *The winning design for Jurong Town Hall*
             was by Architects Team 3.

The authors and publisher apologise to Architects Team
3 for the above errors.

p. 81.   *Chartered Bank Building (top),*
         Hongkong & Shanghai Banking Corpn
         (bottom).

CONTENTS

PICTURE ACKNOWLEDGEMENTS

Archives and Oral History Department.
pp. 13, 15, 35, 44, 46, 59, 62, 68, 76,
78, 79, 80, 81, 83, 84, 85, 86, 88, 89, 97,
98, 99, 116, 118, 126, 127, 133, 134,
136, 142, 143.

Mr. Galsuan. p. 99.

India Office Library. pp. 18, 23, 42.

A. F. Kersting. pp. 22, 23, 38.

National Museum. pp. 8, 10, 11, 15, 16,
18, 26, 27, 28, 29, 33, 34, 37, 40, 42, 45,
54, 55, 57, 59, 61, 62, 63, 65, 67, 94,
116, 118, 119, 131, 141, 143, 146, 162.

Palmer and Turner. pp. 79, 148, 151.

Singapore Land. p. 177.

Simon Winchester. pp. 20, 38, 40.

ACKNOWLEDGEMENTS

So many people have helped and encouraged us throughout the last two years that we would like to record our appreciation.

Firstly, thanks go to the Friends of the National Museum Study Group on Singapore Architecture, 1984, who helped with ideas and research. The members were Sue Sismondo, Susan Dunn, Raija Choa, Barbara Earman, Pat Braig-McFeely, Julia Oh, Jane Robertson, Mr. Lee, and Elizabeth Brown. Elizabeth Brown was kind enough to sketch a Malay house for us. Jo Rider, also a member, has helped enormously with her excellent photographs and has given freely of her time and enthusiasm. Margaret Sullivan steered us through the mine field of book design, and Kheng Choo Campbell of Graham Brash Publishers was ever patient with mistakes and delays.

Mr. Paul Yap, Mr. Andrew Tan, Mr. Kuan Yeu Keng and Mr. Koh Seow Chuan have generously allowed us to reproduce photographs of early Singapore from their collections, as have Mr. Simon Winchester and Mr. A.F. Kersting of buildings in Britain and India. The staff of the India Office Library, the Archives and Oral History department, and Miss Ng Wan Leng of the National Museum have all been of great assistance. Mr. Richard Ng developed photographs at lightening speed, for which we are most grateful.

Mr. Tony Hancock allowed us to pick his brains and photostat articles from his collection, for which we thank him, and Mr. Michael Sweet offered useful suggestion and contacts. Mr. William Lim, Mr. Koh Seow Chuan and Mr. Ong Chin Bee pointed us in the right direction with the modern section.

Personal friends have been wonderful in looking after our children, so that we had peaceful homes for writing and free time for research. Our thanks to all of you for being so understanding.

Above all, we are enormously grateful to our families; parents, husbands and children, who have been drafted in as researchers, copy editors, messengers and sounding boards, and who have done it all in such good humour. They have made the experience a happy one.

Jane Beamish
Jane Ferguson
Singapore May 1985

Vue de la Ville et du detroit de Sincapour, colour lithograph, c. 1840

THE FOUNDATIONS
1819 — 1823

From the time that Thomas Stamford Raffles dropped anchor off the South East coast of Singapore on the 28th of January 1819, to the handover of the island from the East India Company to the Colonial Office on 1st April 1867, the face of Singapore had undergone several radical changes. From a small Malay fishing village with a population of a few hundred, living in attap huts straggled along the coast and up the rivers, the population in 1867 stood at 80,000 to 90,000 comprised mostly of Chinese, Malays, Indians, and Europeans, living in a comparatively well organized and structured city, with amenities for health, education, commerce, leisure and worship; and this not only for the ruling population, but multiplied four and often more times to cater for the demands of Singapore's polyracial society.

Sir Thomas Stamford Raffles was directly responsible not only for the founding of Singapore, but also for the vigorous planning of the young city. Col. William Farquhar, who had been Resident of Malacca during the British interregnum there from 1813 to 1818, was left in charge of Singapore as Resident, with responsibility to Raffles as Lieutenant-Governor in Bencoolen and ultimately to the Governor-General of the East India Company in Calcutta. This was during the period of the Napoleonic wars, when the British East India Company took temporary possession of the Dutch colonies in the East Indies, which included Malacca and Bencoolen. Initially a staunch supporter and friend of Raffles, it was Farquhar who was responsible for Singapore's earliest days, and who, acting on often impractical instructions from an absent Raffles, shaped the early town. By the time Raffles returned in May 1819 for his second visit to the island, land had been cleared and the town sported a busy market and a temporary cantonment for the small garrison on the North East bank of the main river. During this second visit, Raffles outlined the blue print of the future city.

Under the terms of the East India Company's agreement with Sultan Hussein and his chief minister, the Temenggong Abdu'r Rahman, who were the two Malays with whom Raffles negotiated the trading rights on the island, the boundaries of the settlement stretched from Tanjong Katong in the East to Tanjong Malang in the West, and were to reach as far inland as the range of a cannon shot. With his initial plans for the town, Raffles allocated the area to the North of the river for official purposes and for the cantonment. The Temenggong's camp was also on this bank, as were the first European private residences. These were to be sited to the East of the official quarter. Further East again was to be the Sultan's private allotment, in the area known as Kampung Glam. The Chinese quarter, however, was sited on the oppo-

'Partie de Quartier Malais', 1850, colour
engraving, (top)

'River Kampung' by E. Schluter, 1858, water
colour, (bottom)

*'View of Singapore from the Sea', after
Lieut P. Jackson, 1823, pencil*

site marshy South bank of the river and a
bridge was to be built to join the two
sides. The commercial section, Raffles
decided, was to be along the East coast.

The population of the island grew
quickly in these early years. The Malay
and Indonesian communities expanded
with additions not only from Malacca and
Riau, but also from as far afield as
Bencoolen, hence Kampung Bencoolen.
Fierce Bugis seamen, natives of the
Celebes Islands, who were unhappy with
the Dutch trading controls in the area,
came and settled with their families, and
were given an area by Farquhar on the
Rochore river, East of the Sultan in
Kampung Glam. The Chinese, who already had a small presence in Singapore
on Raffles' arrival, came from virtually
every other city in South East Asia, as
well as from the Southern ports of China.
They settled in their allotted area on the
South bank of the Singapore river, and it
swelled to bursting point. Other smaller
communities, like the Armenians and the
Arabs, were also attracted by new trading
possibilities. Neither group were strangers
to this part of the world, as Arabs had
plied their wares to South East Asia for
hundreds of years, and in doing so had
strongly influenced the customs and religions of the area. The Armenians, to a
much smaller extent, were already influential as merchants in several towns.
The third largest immigrant group were
the Indians, who were mostly to begin
with from the Southern parts of the con-
tinent, and in the pay of the East India
Company as soldiers or petty officials. A
few, however, were merchants from the
sizeable Indian community in Penang, the
most notable being Naraina Pillai, who
arrived in the same ship with Raffles on
his second visit to the island in 1819. Pillai
started the first Singapore brick company,
an operation that was to make him not
only rich but a fundamental contributor
to the history of Singapore's early architecture.

Until its return to the Dutch East India
Company after the British interregnum,
Bencoolen had been used by the British
East India Company as a penal colony for
Southern Indian convicts. Both Penang
and Malacca were also used for this purpose, but not to the same extent. On the
return of Bencoolen to the Dutch in 1822,
the convicts were shipped, not back to
India, but to the new settlement of
Singapore. These convicts, mostly
Tamils, were an invaluable source of free
labour during the early years of building,
and at the end of their sentence were given
the option either to return to India, or

stay and settle in Singapore with a small gratuity.

With the various large contingents of different nationalities that made Singapore their home during the first few years, the exception would have to be the Europeans. Apart from officials who worked directly for the East India Company, very few Europeans appeared on the scene at this early stage. The majority of these were representatives of the large Calcutta trading companies, who hastened in to take advantage of the benefits of free trade. But among these Europeans were a few names that have survived throughout the island's history: Alexander Laurie Johnston, who founded the firm A. L. Johnston and Company; Alexander Guthrie, the founder of one of Singapore's largest, and until 1983, its most enduring company. The attitude of Europeans in India and other towns in South East Asia was one of "wait and see", as opinion differed on whether the East India Company would keep Singapore as a permanent possession in the face of strident Dutch opposition. Until this crucial problem was decided, Raffles stipulated that no land grants should be given.

In the event, Farquhar, under pressure from the merchants, was unable to contain this necessary adnuct to expansion, and provisional land grants were given for warehouses and office premises. However, the earliest godowns were not built where Raffles had envisioned them, along the East coast, but on land on the Chinese South bank of the Singapore River. Merchants complained that the East coast approach was too shallow and riddled with sandbanks to be of any use as a landing area. The only proviso that Farquhar gave on the South bank site was a warning that merchants might well have to move later, and that if they insisted on erecting brick buildings to protect their goods from the risk of fire, it was to be on their own heads if they were asked to demolish them within a few years.

Needless to say, with these conditions, the buildings would in no way be described as architectural masterpieces. Elsewhere, the main building materials were wood and attap, the wood being mostly imported, and the attap locally made from dried nipah palm leaves. On his second visit in 1819, Raffles arrived from Penang in a ship laden with timber and tiles, and erratic supplies such as this enabled the town to grow.

When Raffles returned for his third and final visit in October 1822 enroute for England, he was a dejected and bitterly sad man. He had buried three of his four young children in Bencoolen during the previous year, and had seen his ambitious career plans deferred by complicated political wranglings in Calcutta and London. He was in no mood to accept many of the measures that Farquhar had made in his absence and without referral to him. He forced the "King of Malacca", as Farquhar was nicknamed, to resign, and took over himself as Resident, without giving Farquhar any merit for having steered the colony through its earliest and most perilous years.

He immediately embarked on his final plan for the layout of the town, which has endured, albeit with expansion and some change, up to today. An idealist, he laid out "his" city with care and foresight. Aided and abetted by the young Lieutenant Jackson, the Garrison Engineer, and a Town Planning Committee which he formed in November 1822, he segregated the various nationalities that had flocked to Singapore in the preceding two years since his last visit, and for whom he had not made adequate provision. He specified the area for Government buildings, for religious worship, for commerce, education, and even the site for a Botanic Garden, which was a project close to his heart. His master plan for Singapore also

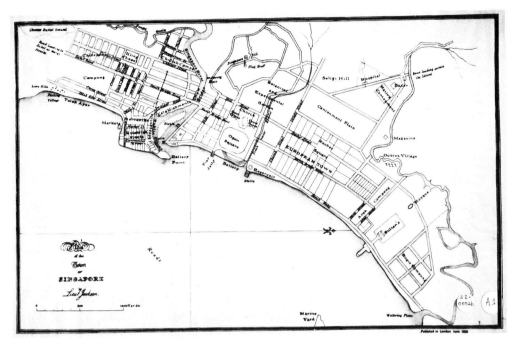

Plan of the Town of Singapore, by Lieut. P. Jackson, 1822

included such details as house size, street widths, and type of materials to be used.

His first problem was with the Temenggong's camp, which had grown in his absence, and existed with its own laws and regulations right in the heart of the proposed Government area. He solved this with persuasion and tact, along with a gift of 5,000 Spanish dollars and the camp was successfully moved out to the West coast, along the area from Tanjong Pagar to Telok Blangah, with the Temenggong setting up camp happily at the base of the subsequently named Mount Faber.

The commercial area posed another problem. Raffles now realized that his previous plan to site it along the East coast was impractical, as the merchants had demonstrated, but the area where many of them had already set up shop on the South and also the North bank of the River, allowed no room for expansion, and indeed on the North bank encroached on the Government quarter, as had the

Temenggong's Kampung. He decided to move the whole lot of them over to the South side, and created a focal point in the form of Commercial Square (now known as Raffles Place), by levelling a hill. The excess dirt from the hill was used to fill in the swamp adjacent to it so that the merchants could expand onto it. It is now known as South Boat Quay.

This all meant, however, that the Chinese quarter, which had previously taken root in the same place, had to be moved further along the coast and up-river, a task that was accomplished at times by force, although payments were made, and free land offered to those who were inconvenienced. The Indians were allotted land North of the Chinese section, and also out to the North of Kampung Glam, beyond the Rochore River.

All the major ethnic areas were designated primarily for the poor, and not for the well-to-do, who could live according to their means and taste, anywhere. Raffles envisaged the Rochore Plain, to the East of the Government quarter, as the place where Asians and Europeans alike could live in affluent and spacious houses. In the commercial section too, different nationalities were encouraged to mix and not split into racial colonies. In the first few years, merchants, be they Chinese, European or Indian, lived side by side above their business premises. The area to the East of the Rochore Plain was also reorganized, and the Arabs and Bugis were shifted further along the East coast to accommodate the expansion. The Sultan's plot at Kampung Glam, however, remained where it was.

* * * * *

Having settled the grand plan for area allotment, Raffles then went on to lay down specific building regulations. He realized that restrictions were needed if the town was to grow in an organized and aesthetic way. As from 1823 land could be purchased at auction on a permanent lease, and because of this, plot purchasers were now willing to spend money on their buildings, instead of making do with flimsy structures. Raffles regulated that in the town areas, roads flanked with houses were to run in intersecting straight lines, and were to be of a specified width. The house plots were also of a specific width, and the buildings were to be no more than three storeys high. Commercial buildings were to be constructed of brick with tiled roofs, and were to be given a solid brick or stone foundation. The five foot way, an arcaded covered walk running along the front of all commercial buildings, was obligatory to protect people from the effects of the weather, and also provide shelter for the small stalls and hawker businesses that were unable to afford premises. The facades of the buildings were to be generally uniform in character.

With these stringent regulations, the typical town architecture of Singapore

took shape. Little if anything survives from this time, and very little was documented about the early Chinatown, but from early paintings one can see neat terraced rows of shop houses and residences, built in stuccoed brick, with red Chinese tiled roofs, and with the characteristic gable and interlocking tiles in a graceful curve over the obligatory five foot way. The facades of the terraces were plain with little or no ornament; perhaps the Chinese bat grill windows decorated the space above the two windows flanking the central door. As the plots were narrow, the houses were long and narrow, often three or four interconnecting rooms deep. In the centre of the houses, it was customary to have an airwell, open to the sky. These were essential for light and ventilation, as the early Chinatown houses backed onto one another with no rear lane or exit. The airwells were also used for water collection and storage, and large jars were placed around them to catch the rain water. All refuse and night soil was collected, unhygienically, from the front. This standard type of Chinese terraced house is common to all parts of South East Asia, and also to Southern ports in China, such as Canton and Macau.

The Malays in their kampungs, preferred to stick to their time honoured tradition of building in wood and attap, as early paintings of Kampung Rochore and Telok Blangah show. Though their houses may appear flimsy and unsubstantial, the Malays and other indigenous people of this region are superb carpenters who understand the aesthetics and strengths of various timbers. The timber, preferably chengai, is good-looking, hard and durable, with a natural white ant proof oil. It is used in thin sections, with careful joinery, for flooring and supports, and in some cases walls as well. The alternative to wood wall panelling is woven thatch made from a combination of

Vue Prise a Sincapour colour lithograph, *1840, (top)*

'Singapore: the South Part of the Town', by *J.T. Thomson, 1846, watercolour, (bottom)*

several different materials, such as rumbia and nibong palm, or bamboo cut in different ways.

The several styles of Malay house all share the same elements of construction, but are laid out differently according to their district. All were built to be movable, and so in a traditional house, no nails or bolts can be found, only timber dowls and wedges. The houses are raised above the ground on stone or timber supports and this acts not only as a defence against flood, animals, insects and evil spirits, but also increases ventilation through the spaces between floor-boards, and makes housekeeping simplicity itself, as crumbs and dust are swept through to the penned chickens and livestock below.

The layout of Malay houses differs again according to the region and preference of the builder, but most comprise a verandah, reception room, visitors' sleeping room, main family living section, and a kitchen at the back. There are usually stairs at the front and back, and the windows are shuttered and sited low on the walls, so those seated at floor level inside can see out. The roofs are high and made from dried and woven attap palms. Decorative features are found on the geometrically woven wall panels, and on the carved wooden fascia boards under the eaves.

The Malay houses found in early Singapore were generally very simple, both in layout and decoration, and reflected the origins and life style of their inhabitants, but one style began to predominate over the years. Called the *rumah bumbong Lima*, it has five separate roof portions which gather over the main section of the house. With a front porch and

Rumah Bumbong Lima, contemporary drawing by Elizabeth Brown, (top)

Government House. Detail from 'Singapore River', c. 1843-7, colour lithograph, (bottom)

either a central stair entrance, or two flanking ones, it has become the most recognizable type of Malay house, and has exerted considerable influence over the detached house architecture in Singapore, which will be explained in greater detail later.

It is perhaps rather significant that when Raffles visited Singapore for the third and final time in 1822, he chose to build himself a wooden Malay style house for the duration of his stay. In fact it remained in service as the Governor's House right up until 1858, when the military took over the hill to fortify it. After Raffles' long experience of the East, he was well qualified to judge what type of building was the most comfortable in which to live. He sited his house on Bukit Larangan, renamed in Raffles' time as Government Hill, and later as Fort Canning. This hill was sacred to the Malays, and was used as a Royal burial ground. For a man very much in touch with the customs and habits of the Malays, it was strange for Raffles to build on sacred land. It has been suggested that after the physical and mental exhaustion of the previous year, he had what would be termed as a death wish, and a desire to be buried among the ancient kings of Singapura, the Lion City. He wrote in a letter to his friend, the orientalist, William Marsden in 1923, "The Tombs of the Malay Kings are, however, close at hand, and I have settled that if it is my fate to die here, I shall take my place among them."

Whatever his reason for building there, it was certainly practical. Singapore then, unlike today, had few large trees to give shade or coolness, and so the site, raised above the heat of the plain and facing into the sea breeze, afforded the greatest comfort. It was one storey of "one hundred feet front and fifty deep" with verandahs spread the length of it to give shade and protection from the rain. Built of wood

and attap roofed, with Venetian louvered windows, it was described by a contemporary traveller as being "so unsubstantial, that after a Sumatra squall has passed over the town, inquiring glances are cast up by the inhabitants to discover whether the house still remains in status quo."

The other Europeans, however, after the first few years, did not follow Raffles' example of choosing wood and attap for their houses. Instead, down on the plain in front of Government Hill, they built spacious brick and stucco houses, facing seawards across the Esplanade, or Padang as it is now known. These they built in the same style as the European houses in Calcutta, Madras and Penang. The man responsible for many of these houses was Singapore's first trained architect, George Drumgoolde Coleman, who arrived in Singapore in June 1822, and met Raffles the same year. Coleman, who was Irish from Drogheda, studied architecture in Dublin before travelling extensively throughout Europe, visiting, like many of his generation, the Roman ruins of Pompeii and Herculaneum, and the Renaissance and Baroque glories of Italy and France. He was well versed in the vocabulary of classical architecture by the time he left Europe for Calcutta in 1815, where he found himself in great demand as a residential house architect for the rich merchants of Fort William. In 1819 he was commissioned to design a cathedral for Batavia (now Jakarta), and when his designs were approved by the Dutch Governor General, Baron van der Cappelen, he sailed for Java. Sadly his

'Raffles's House at Pematang Balam, West Sumatra', by Chinese artist, c. 1823, watercolour, (top)

The North part of the town, colour lithograph, c. 1845, (bottom)

project was never carried out, but he remained in Java for a couple of years, presumably working and travelling before coming on to Singapore in 1822. He was then still a young man of 27, full of enthusiasm for the struggling colony, and he was immediately involved in several of the projects envisioned by Raffles in his 1922 Town Plan, such as the swamp reclamation on the South side of the River where the commercial district was to be sited. He is also thought to have assisted Raffles in his design for the first wood and attap Government House on Government Hill, and later added brick and stucco pediments to the house. But his main contributions to Singapore architecture were the houses and public buildings he designed and built in the European Town.

The state of European architecture in India and South East Asia in the early 19th Century was one that had grown partly out of climatic necessity, and partly from influence brought in from Europe by young architects, new pattern books and the desire of Anglo-Indians to be fashionable. Singapore, unfortunately in some ways, was at the tail end of the East India Company's South Asian acquisitions, and as such, received the sum total of two hundred years of building experience in the East, by the settlers and colonizers of India, Indonesia, Penang and Malacca. With such a powerful and historical precedent there was no need to experiment, no need to find an architectural style to suit, and all the architects and builders of Singapore's early edifices had to do was look across at India, and at the splendours of the Raj, and take from it what they wanted.

However, one cannot view the Raj as the sole inspirer of Singapore's early architecture. It is important to understand the state of 19th Century British architecture was well, and the cumulative influences exerted on it. Throughout British

British Deputy High Commissioner's House, Madras, (top)   *The Tollygunge Club, Calcutta, (bottom)*

architectural history, the three main sources of influence were: Greece, for the pure Classical Greek style; Italy, for the Roman, the Renaissance, the Palladian, and the Baroque; Northern Europe, that is France and Germany, for the Gothic, and France again for the fanciful Rococo. Britain did more than just reproduce slavish copies of these styles and instead learnt from them, combined and adapted them to suit her own tastes, and in doing so created her own architecture. Since the Middle Ages, one after another of these architectural styles has been in vogue in Britain, following in the footsteps of Continental architecture, with the Royal Court and the aristocracy leading the way. With the exception of the Gothic and the Rococo, all the other architectural styles are founded on the Classical Greek and its first cousin, the Roman concept of architecture. The principles laid down by Greek and Roman architects over 2,000 years ago became the architectural cornerstone of Western civilization. Without basic knowledge and understanding of these principles, it is impossible to comprehend any of the succeeding architectural styles. The chief authority on these principles is a Roman architect called Vitruvius, who lived in the first Century B.C. He was the author of the oldest and most influential books on architecture. In his *Ten Books on Architecture*, Vitruvius describes the classic principles of symmetry, harmony and proportion, to which every subsequent architect has adhered in the creation of Western architecture.

However, in British Architecture the 19th Century was a conflicting time. With the advent of the industrial revolution, there was a subtle shift in the quality of patronage, away from the well travelled cognoscenti and dilettante aristocracy, whose interest in architecture and art had stimulated the 17th and 18th Century architects to dazzling heights. The typical post-industrial revolution art patron was a factory owner, or a wealthy merchant who was not bound by any previous limitation of "good taste" or by a desire to strike into new territory. He sought in his architecture principles he felt safe with, and the style he commissioned was often an overt declaration of his wealth. 19th Century architects, therefore, to accommodate their clients, became obsessive historians. They were able to build simultaneously in a Greek, Palladian, Gothic, or even a Hindu fashion: the choice was huge, and the appetite seemingly insatiable. This period has justifiably been described as the "fancy-dress ball of architecture". One only has to bear in mind such buildings as the British Museum (Sir Robert Smirke, begun in 1823), and the Royal Pavilion in Brighton (John Nash 1815-21) to understand the breadth of demand, and the width of taste.

But having condemned the early 19th Century patrons for lacking the finesse of their predecessors, they must be commended for their civic-mindedness. For this is the century of public libraries, of hospitals, of concert halls, orphanages, and above all of churches. There had never been such a concentrated effort on the part of the local authorities in Britain and to a lesser extent, the colonies, to educate, to entertain, and to care physically and spiritually for their citizens.

The British in the East mirrored the tastes of their contempories at home. Although separated by several months sailing, and more than several degrees in climate, the rich merchants and officials of the East India Company were determined to have the same or a higher standard of living than they would have enjoyed at home. The 18th Century Calcutta and Madras merchants built themselves spacious square palazzos in stuccoed brick, severe neo-classical blocks, with little or no regard for the

British Museum, London. Sir John Smirke,
1823, (top)

Royal Pavilion, Brighton. John Nash,
1815–21, (bottom)

Chiswick House, Chiswick. Lord Burlington and William Kent, 1720, (top)

Town Hall, Calcutta. Col. John Garton, 1809–13, (bottom)

23

different weather conditions. Few had verandahs or carriage porches, and apart from the solid walls to retain what little coolness there was, the houses must have been intolerable. Gone were the earlier settlers' bamboo roofs and matting walls. In their place stood gleaming classical monuments. The buildings of the British Raj in India were meant to tell a moral tale. They were monuments of rulers, and of a way of life impervious to the riotious and excessive East. "I thought I was no longer in the world I had left in the East" wrote one impressed Malay visiting the Grecian elegance of Calcutta at the end of the 18th Century. Contemptuous of the indigenous culture of India and anything that it might offer — Thomas Macaulay ridiculed Indian history as "abounding with Kings thirty feet high and reigns thirty thousand years long" — the British once even contemplated demolishing the Taj Mahal for its valuable building material, and many Indian buildings, both sacred and secular, were brutally altered "a la style Anglais".

The beginning of the 19th Century saw a change in the style of British architecture in India from the pure neo-classical to the grandeur and dignity of neo-Palladianism. Palladianism, as an architectural style, had already been popular in England as far back as the early 17th Century, with the architect Inigo Jones. It was to make an impact on 19th Century colonial architecture unsurpassed by any other. The application of a classical temple portico on domestic housing, the regimental use of proportion 1.2, 2.2 and the repetitious arrangement of facade decoration became the passwords of British colonial architecture. The 17th and 18th Century British followers of Paduan architect Andrea Palladio were themselves copied slavishly in British India and South East Asia. Palladio's books, *I Quattro Libri dell'Architettura* (Venice, 1570) in which he illustrates and explains many of his buildings, were a must in the libraries of all architects who designed classical buildings. George Coleman was no exception. With his training in Dublin, subsequent tour of Europe, and work experience in classical Calcutta, he arrived in Singapore well grounded in both the original and the copies.

COLEMAN'S LEGACY
1823 — 1841

Early paintings of Singapore bear testament to the enormous influence Coleman exerted on the city's first architectural style. The famous view of the Esplanade by John Turnbull Thomson painted in 1851, after Coleman's death, shows no fewer than six Coleman designed buildings, with the rest following his stylistic dictum.

After his work on Raffles' first Government House, and with the town plan of 1922 which involved large scale drainage and road works, one of the first residential buildings Coleman designed was for a John Argyle Maxwell, a wealthy merchant with business connections in Java, who had been appointed one of the first three magistrates by Raffles in 1823. Maxwell never actually occupied the grandiose mansion Coleman built for him in 1826-7. A combination of constant travelling to and from his estates in Java, followed by an early retirement, and a dispute over his legal right to the land on which the house was built, conspired against him, and he left Singapore for Scotland in the early 1830's, seemingly unaffected by his inability to reside in Coleman's earliest masterpiece.

The house (now the Parliament Building), was built on the North East bank of the Singapore River, and occupied perhaps the most historic site on the island. It was here, directly on the building's river frontage that Raffles was presumed to have landed on 29th January, 1819, and it was also here and in the area running up to the High Street, that the Temenggong had built his Kampung, with his own house very near to the site where Maxwell's house was subsequently built. In his vision of the developing Singapore, Raffles had directed that this particular area should be reserved for Government purposes only, and once the Temenggong and his followers were persuaded to move out to Telok Blangah, the Kampung was demolished and the site prepared for building.

But before any Government building could be started, John Crawfurd who had taken over from Raffles as Resident, issued a permit for Maxwell to build a private residence on the site. After the house was completed in 1827, the trouble started. Maxwell applied for a statutory grant to the site, and John Prince, Crawfurd's successor, referred the matter to the Governor in Calcutta, explaining that Maxwell should never have been allowed to occupy the plot in the first place, as this was land appropriated for Government use. Calcutta's reply to Maxwell was equitable. Since Maxwell had gone to the expense of building a large and expensive residence "it would be unreasonable to deprive you of the advantages to which you may be entitled by the possession of this valuable lot ....." On that note Maxwell was granted a 999 year lease, and in the same spirit Maxwell offered the house back to the Government

'The Padang in Singapore'
by J.T. Thomson, 1851, oil on canvas,
(top)

Detail from 'View of Singapore Town from
Government Hill', 1846, colour lithograph,
(bottom)

*Detail from 'The First Court House'
(Parliament House) by Lieut. Begbie 1834,
watercolour*

for official use at an annual rent of 500 rupees.

From then on it became known as the Court House. Until 1875 it housed the Public Offices of the Settlement, and on the hand over of the island to the Colonial Office, the Supreme Court. When the new Supreme Court was completed in 1939, the house became semi-derilect and was declared unsafe, and for many years was used as a store house, and as an office for the newly created Department of Social Welfare. It was given a new lease of life, however, by Sir John Nicholl, Governor of Singapore in 1953, who initiated renovations and rebuilding, and in 1954 on completion, it opened as the New Assembly House. It is today the Parliament House, a far cry from the proposed palatial residence of one John Argyle Maxwell, merchant of Singapore, but a fitting reminder of the continuity of Government in Singapore, and a direct link to Raffles' vision.

Very little remains of the early building, but in its original form, it was perhaps Coleman's finest piece of residential architecture, and a dignified and impressive start to his career in Singapore. On two floors, the front portico had a heavily colonnaded Roman Doric pier base rising to an Ionic supported triangular pediment. The three storeyed watchtower on the river elevation had the same weighty pier base, but was decorated above with slender Ionic columns. The four corners of the building were punctuated by pairs of columns, and the windows were neatly defined and repetitive. Behind a simple balustrade on the riverfront tower, a small pair of cupolas completed the house. The hybrid of styles that Coleman used in the design of the house is intriguing to unravel. In essence it was a Palladian derivative, with all the attendant details: the ground floor rustication, the strong delineation of the floors, and the impressive entrance portico, erroneously thought by Palladio to be *de riguer* in Roman domestic architecture and used by him and his British followers on virtually every opportunity — all very well in the strong Italian, and even stronger Singapore sun, but decidely drafty in the British long winter. In feeling, however, the house had subtler influences. The strong piers supporting the portico and the two columned floors on the riverside front, were perhaps more British than Italian in origin. The chief 18th Century British exponent of Palladio was the architect Colin Campbell (1676–1729), who, with the publication of two volumes in 1715 and 1717 entitled *Vitruvius Britanicus*, and the subsequent translation

*Front view of Mr. Maxwell's House
(Parliament House). G.D. Coleman,
1826–27, (top)*

*River view of Mr. Maxwell's House
(Parliament House). G.D. Coleman,
1826–27, (bottom)*

Side elevation of the Supreme Court   *Parliament House today, (bottom)*
(Parliament House) after Improvements,
1875, (top)

Elevation of the Right Honourable the Lord Herbert his House in Whitehall.

into English of Palladio's *I Quattro Libri dell' Architettura*, spearheaded the 18th Century Palladian movement in Britain.

It is in several of Campbell's designs for houses (notably Lord Herbert's house in Whitehall, built in 1723-4 and now demolished) that one can see where Coleman's inspirations lie. The flavour of Calcutta is also there, and there would be no difficulty in assimilating Maxwell's house into the Tollygunge area of the city, where more Palladian inspired mansions abound per square foot than in any other city East of Suez. One can almost be certain that every Coleman building in Singapore has a close relative in either Calcutta or Madras. Maxwell's house has now, of course, changed out of all recognition. It was remodelled and extended by Captain McNair, Colonial Engineer in 1874-5, who retained much of Coleman's original intention, but then in 1901 it was again remodelled, this time not so sensitively. After the extensive renovations in 1953 the building today retains little of George Coleman's hand on the exterior or interior.

Another fine residential building by Coleman is now part of the Convent of the Holy Infant Jesus. It was commissioned in 1840-41 by a Mr Caldwell, the Senior Magistrate's clerk. Mr Caldwell had better luck than Mr Maxwell, and inhabited his house for a good ten years before it was bought over in 1852 by Father Beurel, who opened a girls' school in the house in 1854. Less imposing than Mr Maxwell's· house, this smaller house nevertheless has the clear hallmarks of Coleman's style. As has been mentioned, it is unlikely that any of Coleman's buildings in Singapore are uni-

que in design, and there is in the Tollygunge in Calcutta a house extremely similar to the one Coleman designed for Mr Caldwell. Coleman, like the architects who followed him, plagiarized freely from the various pattern books available at the time. After the very important and much used Colin Campbell's *Vitruvius Britanicus*, which was a survey of the classical buildings existing in England at the beginning of the 18th Century, there was James Gibbs' *Book of Architecture,* 1828, produced by the architect of St Martin-in-the-Fields in London, and destined to result in a flood of emulative St Martin's all over the colonies, Singapore included. More up-to-date architectural pattern books, as far as Coleman and his successors were concerned, were by John Loudon in the 1830's. These contained, in the form of encyclopaedias, models for almost every kind of building, in whatever style, and were exceptionally popular and well thumbed by the colonial builders. Plagiarism, therefore, was not the dirty word it is now. The Roman, Renaissance and 18th Century British Palladian architects were masters of proportion and subtle dignity, and the generous and unhurried bow fronted facade of Caldwell's house reflects that knowledge. Coleman's columns are loadbearing and important, his cornices emphatic without being overpowering, and every curve and line plays its part in harmonizing the whole. He is without doubt Singapore's premier architect, as well as the first. He was appointed Singapore's first Superintendent of Public Works in 1833.

Mr Maxwell's and Mr Caldwell's houses are the only two remaining private residences left standing that can definitely be attributed to Coleman. The Kampung Glam Istana, built in the early 1840's, is reputed to be by him, but there is no definite evidence to support the suggestion. It is a straightforward double storey

Lord Herbert's House, London, Colin Campbell, 1723-4, (top)

The Old Madras Club, Madras, (bottom)

Mr. Caldwell's House, Victoria Street.
G.D. Coleman, 1840–41, (top)

Aildeen, Calcutta,
(bottom)

Istana, Kampung Glam, 1840's

squared house with a central arched carriage porch in front. Its heavy overhanging double eaves, louvred windows, with balustrades behind them on the upper floor, and simple but strong delineation of the floors and carriage porch arches, is of a type well known in India, and subsequently much used here in Singapore. It differs from the main stream of this style of house by being decidedly better and more generously proportioned than most, which perhaps betrays Coleman's hand in the design. It is sited right in the heart of Kampung Glam on the Sultan's walled estate, granted to him by Raffles, and is still lived in by his descendants. It is painted a rather strong shade of yellow, the colour of Kings the world over.

Coleman's own house, in Coleman Street, and many more that he built for the first merchant settlers have all given way to the developers, and we are forced to rely on paintings, old photographs, and eye-witness reports for representation. Number Three Coleman Street,

Coleman's home from 1829 for twelve years, was another example of his intolerance of the second rate. A substantial house of three storeys, made of brick and stucco as were all the houses he designed, the building was encircled with giant order double pilasters set on tall plinths. The front was columned, not pilastered, and the entire width was a carriage porch. The roof was in two layers, the gap between the two layers allowing light into the small top rooms and the semi-circular clerestory windows of the dining room. This room was the most significant in the house and indeed in Singapore at that time. The walls were inset with rectangular panels with moulded architraves, some with large oil paintings hanging in them, and the moulded entablature frieze above them had delightful references to Coleman's nationality, with intertwined harps and shamrocks. The panels of the room, if not decorated by paintings were painted different colours, and these contrasted with the gleaming whiteness of the Madras chunam walls. The ceiling was timber, and the floor was laid with red Malacca tiles. This splendid dining room and also the dining room in Maxwell's house, Coleman positioned on the first

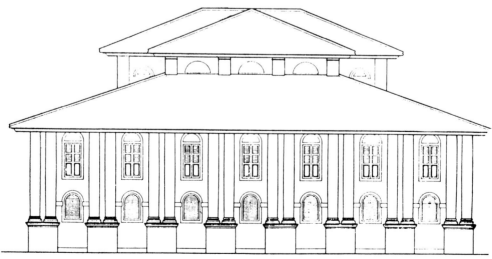

Coleman's House, 3 Coleman Street.
G.D. Coleman, 1829, (top left)

Front elevation of 3 Coleman Street.
G.D. Coleman, 1829, (bottom left)

3 Coleman Street in the 1950's, (top)

Dining Room, 3 Coleman Street.
G.D. Coleman, 1829, (bottom)

floor, which is a feature of some Palladian houses. The treatment of the inset panels and the clerestory windows is very similar in both houses.

One practicality that much hampered builders and architects in early Singapore was the lack of building materials, skilled workers and — perhaps not so much in the case of private residences as with Government buildings — the lack of money. But thanks to the likes of Mr Pillai from Penang, who set up the first brickworks, and the increasing supplies of Indian Tamil convict labour for construction work, these problems were to some extent resolved. The convicts were marshalled for construction work under the watchful and efficient eyes of a series of Superintendents of Convicts, and were themselves a useful source of inventive measures to conceal deficiencies of building materials. A substance called Madras chunam, for instance, which was used instead of plaster on walls all over India, was also easy to manufacture in Singapore with local ingredients. This concoction is a mixture of shell lime, egg white, a coarse sugar called jaggery, and water which has had coconut husks soaked in it. When this was applied to brick walls and polished with a rounded stone, or piece of rock crystal, it shone beautifully, and was exceptionally hard wearing. It was used extensively for interior walls. If expensive materials were needed, they were imported. The teak came from Burma, marble from China, and stone from Indonesian quarries as well as Pulau Ubin. The Dutch, and subsequently the British in Malacca, had always used brick for building rather than stone, and as this was in more ready supply, Singapore followed suit.

Coleman left Singapore in 1841 and was on home sick leave until 1843. His house and the contents were sold to the energetic and charismatic hotel owner, Gaston Dutronquoy, who set up the London Hotel on the premises. In 1843 he also started Singapore's first Repertory Company, the Theatre Royal, on the ground floor. The Hotel was moved out in 1845 to two other houses facing the Esplanade that Coleman had designed on the site of the present Supreme Court, and the name was changed to the Hotel de l' Europe, destined to be one of the finest in the East. Coleman's house changed names as frequently as the years, and became successively the first Adelphi Hotel (subsequently moved), the Hotel de la Paix, the Metropole and finally the Burlington Hotel. In 1863 the verandahs were filled in, and further degeneration took place during the Second World War and the Japanese occupation, when shops were built into the verandahs. The house was finally pulled down in 1970 to make way for the Peninsula Shopping Centre; not a happy ending for Singapore's first architect's home.

Coleman's Saint Andrews Church suffered the same fate over a hundred years earlier, but for reasons beyond his control. The spire, which was not designed by Coleman but by J. T. Thomson, an architect and surveyor who worked in Singapore during the 1840's and 50's, was struck by lightning twice, and consequently the whole building suffered and was declared unsafe. The church was demolished in 1855. Coleman designed two churches during his career in Singapore. St. Andrews was completed in 1836, and the Armenian Church, which is sited a short distance away, a year earlier in 1835.

Land had been allocated in Raffles' Town Plan of 1822 for an Anglican church, but for many years nothing had been done about a suitable place of worship for the Anglican community, and they conducted services in a small overcrowded chapel built by the Rev. Thompson. In 1834 contributions from the local community were obtained and

St. Andrew's Church. G.D. Coleman,
1835–36. Detail from 'Vue de Temple
Protestant', 1837, colour lithograph, (top)

'St. Andrew's Church with Spire',
by J.T. Thomson, 1842, watercolour,
(bottom)

Coleman was appointed architect of a new church which would, in the words of the visiting Archbishop of Calcutta, be "neat, convenient, commodious and elegant". And so St. Andrews was. Coleman designed a fine classical structure facing onto the Esplanade. Rectangular in plan, the front boasted an imposing facade of columns capped by a triangular pediment. A deep 20 foot arched verandah ran around the building on three sides, enclosing the carriage roads. Above the verandah were galleries. A balustrade ran along the roof line. Interestingly, several designs were sent from Calcutta architects for the church, but these were all discarded by the church building committee as none of them took into account the fierce climate of either hot sun, or lashing rain, which Coleman's verandahs did, for they succeeded in keeping the central core of the church both cool and dry.

As with his other buildings, there are several prototypes in the area that Coleman would most certainly have seen and on which he could have loosely based his St. Andrews. St. George's, Penang is a similar porticoed building, as is St. George's Cathedral, Madras, although on a very much grander scale. St. Andrews Church, Calcutta, built by Messrs Burn, Currie and Company in 1815, the year of Coleman's arrival in Calcutta, has many of the features that Coleman subsequently incorporated into the Singapore St. Andrews. As was briefly mentioned, all these churches owe their inspiration to James Gibbs' *Book of Architecture* (1728), and especially to his St. Martin-in-the-Fields 1721-26 which is illustrated in the book, and which is still standing today on the corner of Trafalgar Square in

St. Andrew's Church, Calcutta. Messrs. Burn, Currie and Company, 1815, (top)

St. Martin-in-the-Fields Church, London. James Gibbs, 1721-26, (bottom)

London. Gibbs was not in the mainstream of the 18th Century English Palladian movement. He was one of the most individual of English architects, and he had studied in Rome in the studio of Carlo Fontana. One of the few British architects of the time to have actually studied abroad, instead of just participating in protracted European Grand Tours, he has become the most influential London church architect of the early 18th Century. As we can see in a building like Coleman's St. Andrews, his influence was still very much in force 100 years later.

The spire, which was added by J. T. Thomson in 1842 after grumbling from the Anglican community that the church resembled a "Town Hall a College or an Assembly Room", was in the same simplified Gibbs tradition. It rose from the ridge of the roof directly behind the temple front portico, the central part of which had to be filled in to support the weight.

The small church of St. Gregory the Illuminator, which was commissioned by the first 12 Armenian families to live in Singapore, can, like St. Andrews, be directly linked to designs appearing in James Gibbs' *Book of Architecture*. Commissioned by the Armenian community to be a centrally designed church, as was its mother church at Echiadzin in Northern Armenia, it can firstly be traced back through India with the study of the splendidly massive St. Andrews Scottish Church in Madras, built in 1820 by Thomas de Havilland, and from there, straight back to James Gibbs.

In Coleman's original design which has now been altered, on the external square cross plan, there were three pedimented Tuscan Doric porticos facing North, South and West, and on the East side, no portico, but a beautifully bowed apse decorated with Tuscan Doric pilasters, and an inverted window sequence from the remainder of the building. The long

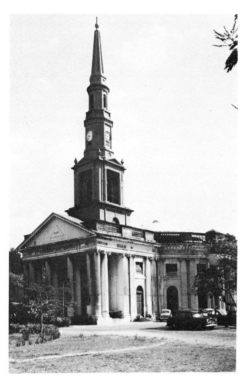

St. Andrew's Church, Madras. Thomas De Havilland, 1820, (top)

St. Gregory the Illuminator. Detail from 'Singapore' by Charles Hamilton Smith, 1840, colour lithograph (bottom)

Church of St. Gregory the Illuminator, Hill Street. G.D. Coleman, 1835, (opposite)

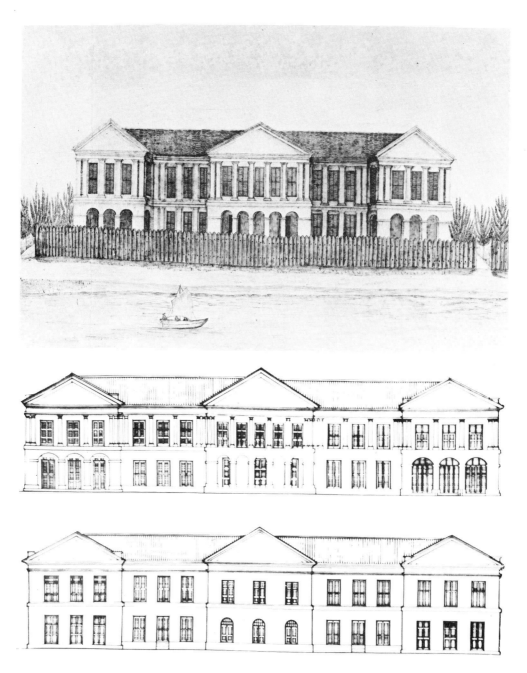

*Front elevation, Singapore Institution
(Raffles Institution), Bras Basah. Lieut.
P. Jackson and G.D. Coleman, 1823-35*

*'The Singapore Institution' by J.A. Marsh,
1841, pen, ink and watercolour,
(bottom)*

oval-topped louvred windows on the ground floor and the totally undecorated rectangular windows above would appear to be the very same type and arrangement as those in St. Andrews Scottish Church in Madras. Coleman's delicate bell turret, which perched above the pitched octagonal roof, was replaced first in 1847 by a square one, and then again in 1853 by the present one. The architect of the spire also replaced the roof, and the bowed East front was boxed in to create another portico on which the spire could rise.

The interior of the church is extremely simple, with recessed windows and doors at intervals around the circular room. The altar is in a small chapel which was mirrored externally by the bowed East front. The roof is planked wood, and is gently domed. Altogether, Coleman's original design for St. Gregory was simple and unfussy. The building, although small in scale, has a monumental quality and yet a freshness of execution, that could well have turned to disaster in the hands of a less competent architect. The Singapore Free Press said of the church on its completion in 1835 that "it was one of the most ornate and best finished pieces of architecture that this gentleman can boast of".

That is more than can be said of another of Singapore's early buildings, the Singapore Institution (later called the Raffles Institution). Started in 1823 by Lieutenant Jackson, the Garrison Engineer who helped Raffles with the Town Plan of 1822 shortly after his arrival in Singapore, it was the fulfilment of Raffles' wish to bring the finest of Western education to the best of South East Asian students in Singapore. The foundation stone was laid only three days before Raffles' final departure from the island, and the site chosen was just across Bras Basah Creek, now called Stamford Canal, virtually on the coastline. Jackson, as architect, chose a very simple style of design. With a rusticated base, and carriage porches projecting front and back with colonnaded piers, this compact core could be repeated as often as necessary. The first storey louvred windows were tall and rectangular, each divided from the next by simple Doric pilasters. The entablature was broad and emphatic, and served to emphasize the clear cut and precise style of architecture.

Jackson's Singapore Institution was never properly finished. After Raffles left the island, Crawford, the next Resident, saw no reason to waste precious government funds in the pursuit of an ideal which he felt premature for Singapore. In a letter to Calcutta in 1826 he writes, "The native inhabitants of Singapore have not yet attained that state of civilization and knowledge which would qualify them to derive advantage from the enlarged system of education held by the Singapore Institution." Work stopped and the building was never used. In the 1830's, visitors to the new thriving port of Singapore were puzzled on being confronted with the semi-complete ruin on the coast, called affectionately Jackson's Ruin by the inhabitants. Just 10 years of disuse had wreaked havoc, and in the words of the Free Press, "for several years it has been an eyesore". In 1835 the money was found by a group of European merchants to complete the Institution, and Coleman was appointed the new architect to finish the building to Jackson's original plan. At last it could be used for what it was intended and fulfil Raffles' wish that it "may be the means of civilizing and bettering the conditions of millions".

Coleman's contribution to the early architecture of Singapore cannot be over emphasized. Not only was he the architect of the majority of the splendid and elegant houses commissioned by the Europeans, but he also built their places of worship and education. He turned his

hand to several smaller commercial projects as well, such as Edward Boustead's godown on the Singapore River which, although demolished in 1925, was copied by Tan Kim Seng in 1851-55 for another godown. That Coleman was able to elevate a mundane warehouse from its everyday function to a building of distinction illustrates his talent extremely well. Facing along the river, where the lighters transferred goods from the ships out in the harbour into the merchants' go-downs, the building had a graceful colonnade of arches, which rose through to the upper storey. Coleman also designed one of the early Telok Ayer markets in 1835, jutting out into Telok Ayer Bay before it was reclaimed. The market was an octagonal building with an inner and outer drum, the outer colonnaded not only to give light to the inner but also to protect it from direct sunlight and rain driving off the bay. Structurally the market was not a great success, and monsoons and sea water took their toll all too quickly. Complaints were made over the years about its safety, but it survived until the present market was built in 1894.

The State of Johore mosque at the base of Mt. Faber, formally the Reception Hall for the Temenggong's Istana, is a similar structure, although little is known of its origin. Both the mosque and the small porticoed shrine close by are fine, well designed buildings, and merit further study.

Coleman's trip home in 1841 for three years sick leave signified the end of his career in Singapore. Although he returned in 1843, he did no further work, and died only three months later of a fever. He was buried in the Fort Canning cemetery, overlooking the city he helped to build.

Tan Kim Seng's Godown, between Elgin and Coleman Bridges, 1851–55, (top)

Telok Ayer Market, Telok Ayer Bay. G.D. Coleman, 1835. Detail from 'Telok Ayer Market' by J.T. Thomson, 1847, watercolour, (top right)

State of Johor Mosque, Telok Blangah Road, (bottom right)

A COMMUNITY SPIRIT
1830 — 1880

The other important buildings of this early period in Singapore's architectural history are mostly religious. As the first immigrants settled, and trade and commerce expanded, the various communities found the time, money and energy to commission permanent places of worship and do away with the initial wood and attap huts that had doubled for temples, mosques and churches in the beginning years.

Few cities other than Singapore can boast of so many major religious buildings all within a few square miles. Each bears witness to the peaceful co-existence of Singapore's various faiths, and each, unique with its own long history of traditional architectural format, represents its worshippers' origins and native culture, far more so than secular buildings which are swayed and altered according to contemporary taste and preference. Structurally, Singapore's religious buildings owe little to one another, and their architecture developed in their countries of origin over thousands of years, for the most part unaware of and unaffected by foreign influence or change. In principle, however, they all reflect the same pur-

Cathedral of the Good Shepherd, Bras Basah. Denis McSwiney, 1843–46, (top)

Interior, Cathedral of the Good Shepherd, Bras Basah. Denis McSwiney, 1843–46, (bottom)

pose; as places of worship where the community can gather to praise and pray to their gods. The only common denominator to be found, is that they owe nothing in their structure to being built in Singapore.

The Anglican and Armenian communities, as we have seen, were fortunate in having an architect such as George Coleman for their respective churches. The Roman Catholic community, however, had an amateur architect design their Cathedral of the Good Shepherd in Bras Basah Road. Prior to that, services were conducted in a small shed built in 1830 on the site of Father Beurel's first school for boys, St. Joseph's Institution.

The Cathedral was built in 1843-6 on the designs of Denis McSwiney, who was by trade a contractor and a general merchant, and whose only other attempt at building was the first Assembly Rooms at the foot of Government Hill on the Hill Street Police Station site. These, to his great shame, were declared unusable after a mere 10 years. It is, therefore, somewhat remarkable, that given his "talents", the Cathedral of the Good Shepherd still stands today. It is a classical building, basilican in ground plan, and owes much to Coleman's influence. It has six porticoed entrances, one at either end, and two on each side, each with an arrangement of rounded and squared Tuscan Doric columns. The church was extended by three bays, in 1888, but has received no other structural alterations. The windows, now glassed, but originally shuttered, are rectangular with oval tops, and extend virtually the height of the wall. Simple Doric pilasters divide them. The interior of the church is plain and unadorned. There are no aisles or columns to create any special relationships, and it suffers in comparison to Coleman's works.

The impressive tower and spire, however, were added in 1847, and were designed by Charles Alexander Dyce, another amateur, but a man of many talents, who visited Singapore from 1842-47 with the trading firm of Martin, Dyce and Company. It is Gibbsian in character, well designed and proportioned, and adds much to the stature of the Church.

Although the second St. Andrews, the present one, was not built until a decade later in 1856-64, it is perhaps worth commenting on now, in the context of Christian churches. Coleman's classical St. Andrews, with the addition of Thomson's spire which proved to be such an unfortunate lightning magnet, was pulled down in 1852, and work commenced on a new church four years later under the supervision of its architect, Col. Ronald MacPherson. Like McSwiney, he was an amateur architect, but a competent engineer, and, like Coleman, he held the important post of Executive Engineer and Superintendent of Convicts from 1855-57. So, as with the majority of Singapore's early buildings, this second St. Andrews was built by Indian convict labour, firstly under MacPherson, and then when he left in 1857, under the the new Executive Engineer and Superintendent of Convicts, Captain J. F. A. McNair, of the Royal Artillery.

MacPherson, the architect for this second St. Andrews, broke new ground in Singapore by choosing to design a Gothic church. He had been impressed in his youth by a 13th Century Gothic Cistercian abbey in Hampshire, called Netley (now ruined), and it was with this in mind that he designed St. Andrews. As was mentioned previously, the 19th Century British architects, and their patrons, saw no discrepancy in choosing at one moment, a classical style of architecture, be it Palladian, Baroque, or Renaissance, and at the next a Gothic, or Romanesque style. Indeed, in the mid 19th Century Englishman's mind, the soaring arches and ethereal pinnacles of Gothic architecture, seemed more in keeping with religious fervour than cool classical monuments, which were after all, pagan in origin, more suited to the worship of Zeus, and plagiarized for Christian use only since the Renaissance. Gothic conjures up visions of Notre Dame, Durham, Canterbury and Chartres, of Christianity in direct and powerful terms, and its popularity in Britain during the mid 19th Century was high. Not only was the burnt Palace of Westminster replaced by the Gothic style Houses of Parliament in 1836 by Pugin and Barry, but out of the 214 churches commissioned and financed all around the British Isles by the Church Building Act of 1818, 174 of them were subsequently built in a Gothic style. It was in this context that MacPherson designed St. Andrews.

However, the Gothic used in a great many of the British churches, and which transmigrated across the world to India and South East Asia, can justly be called "economical" Gothic. The lines are simple, and clear, and there is very little of the fancy decorative element so beloved of the High Gothic Masters of the 12th and 13th Centuries, such as elaborate tracery, abundant rosettes, and richly carved capitals. The economical Gothic typified by St. Andrews is more in keeping with the early English Gothic which relies on clarity of line and form for impact, rather than dazzling detail.

Netley Abbey from the South East,
Hampshire. England. Mid 13th Century,
(top)

Frontispiece: Apology for the Revival of
Christian Architecture in England,
A.W.N. Pugin. 1832, (bottom)

St. Andrew's Cathedral, St. Andrew's Road.
Col. R. MacPherson, 1857. From an
engraving, Illustrated London News, 1866,
(top)

Interior, St. Andrew's Cathedral,
St. Andrew's Road.
Col. R. MacPherson, (bottom)

The principal entrance of the basilican Cathedral of St. Andrews, lies under the vault of the two storey tower on which the spire rises. In MacPherson's original plans, the tower was to have been double in height, with no spire, but during the building, it was discovered that the foundations of the church would not stand the strain of so heavy a structure, and so the design was changed to incorporate the present, light spire. The nave, which runs uninterrupted the length of the Cathedral is flanked by the North and South dasles, and separated from them by a series of narrow bays, which lead the eye through the chancel arch into the Nativity Chapel. The compound piers of the bays are well proportioned and have plain unadorned capitals. The arches are high and pointed. The clerestory windows, reflecting the pointed arches of the bays and aisle windows, are flanked by pairs of pilasters and are simply decorated with intersecting tracery and coloured glass. The roof is of timber.

It is the East and West ends of the Cathedral that are the most decorated. Sadly, the original stained glass windows of the East end were destroyed during the Second World War, although they had been carefully taken down and stored, but the effect remains the same. With the two nigh arches leading into the Nativity Chapel, they dominate the length of the church and play on the harmony of arches within arches. The central light, or window, is dedicated to the memory of Raffles, the North to John Crawfurd, and the South to Major General William Butterworth, who was Governor from 1843-55, and who instigated the building of this second St. Andrews.

At the opposite end, the West end, is the gallery, which was not part of MacPherson's plan but which was erected after the Cathedral was opened. It possesses the only ornament found in the church, with foliated pillars and pilasters, and crocketed arches.

The North and South transepts, which were originally built as carriage porches, have since been extended in the original style to provide offices and meeting halls. The Church was consecrated as a Cathedral in 1870.

The Gothic Revival of St. Andrews marked the beginning of a trend, and several future churches were designed in the same style. St. Peter and Paul, in Queen Street, 1871, Our Lady of Lourdes in Ophir Road, 1888, by Swan and Maclaren, and the Chapel of the Holy Infant Jesus, attached to Mr Caldwell's house, 1910 by Father Nain, are all examples of 19th Century Gothic Revival.

The other Singapore church that expresses individuality in its architecture is the small, but handsome Presbyterian church at the top of Stamford Road. Built slightly later than the other churches mentioned, it warrants studying for its finely designed facade. A small chapel had existed on the site for several years before building started on the church in 1877, and prior to that the congregation had been welcomed at St. Andrews. The main entrance at the West end has a curious mixture of styles. The dominant feature is a Serlian motif, more commonly known as a Palladian window. This is an archway with three openings, the central one arched and the two flanking with straight entablature. Used in classical Rome, it was reintroduced by 16th Century architects, especially Palladio, and it is in his work, and the work of his devoted British followers, that you mostly see it. Here on the Presbyterian church, there are double Ionic columns supporting the arch of the porch, which is echoed above a smaller version on the actual facade. The small cupola that tops the facade rests on a circular arched colonnade. One nice touch are the volutes, or scrolls, that rise from the entablature either side of the central arch of the carriage porch. These volutes

Tan Si Chiong Su Temple, Magazine Road. 1876

or burned easily, but wall paintings, and *ming-chi* (pottery funerary furniture) have survived, and archaeological excavations have revealed that even from the very beginning of Chinese history, the architecture was based on the strength of the column, not the walls.

The pagoda is also a dominant form in Chinese architecture. Originally introduced into China from India along with the advent of Buddhism during the Tang Dynasty, the Chinese quickly assimilated it, and modified it to their own taste. Chinese pagodas are usually built on a square plan with successive storeys of diminishing width, with each storey supporting its own curved roof on prominent and elaborately carved brackets. Hexagonal or octagonal plans, such as the two pagodas in Thian Hock Keng, were also popular at different times, especially during the Sung period.

Tan Si Chiong Su Temple in Magazine Road, is another fine architectural example, small, but perfectly balanced. Financed by the son of Tan Tock Seng, Tan Kim Ching, it was built as an assembly hall for the Tan Clan in 1876, and possesses some excellent examples of granite pillars, carved with writhing dragons. These, along with other decorative elements, were imported from China. The flamboyant style of decoration in most of the Chinese temples in Singapore, reflects the tastes of the Southern Chinese who formed the majority of Singapore's early immigrants: the Hokkien, Teochew and Hakkas. Northern Chinese temples are considerably more restrained and austere compared to their Southern cousins, whose exuberance reached a peak during the Ching Dynasty. Singapore's early temples, therefore, with their exaggerated forms and gaudy colours represent the height of the Southern style.

It is interesting for Westerners to learn the symbolic meanings the Chinese attach

Dragon Column, Tan Si Chiong Su Temple, Magazine Road. 1876

to colours and animal and plant forms, for many are in direct confrontation with Western myths and legends. The dragon, for instance, has, in Western Art, always been the symbol of Evil, and much emphasis has been placed on its defeat and death by the courage of the forces of Good. The Chinese, however, view the dragon through different eyes. It is for them synonymous with strength, and justice, and a guardian of the wishes of the gods as well as an imperial emblem. There is also a strong connection between dragons and the water element, so the roof ridges of Thian Hock Keng and numerous other Singapore temples, which are decorated with many pairs of dragons chasing the central flaming pearl of immortality, are a fitting reminder of the early Chinese immigrants who risked dangerous sea voyages to settle on

Singapore shores. Colour plays a key role in temple *fung shui* or Chinese geomancy, and the vigour and festivity of red is combined with royal gold or yellow, to represent power and glory. Green, signifying longevity, is often used for the floor tiles as it is a natural earth colour.

In the same way that Greek and Roman architecture has permeated every form in Western architecture, Chinese architects and builders are bound to follow the strict principles of Yin and Yang, and the complicated nuances of Chinese geomancy. To do otherwise, especially in the building of a temple, would be to court disaster, and even in the 1980's, when skyscrapers are the rule, not the exception, the Chinese still hold to these ancient and well tried principles.

The Muslims who arrived in Singapore during the first decades came from three main sources. The most numerous were the Indian Muslims from the Southern states, known as the Chulias. The poorer Chulias were settled north of the Chinese town, in the area around Chulia and Market Streets, and were mostly small traders. Other Indian Muslims were assimilated into the Arab-Malay area of Kampung Glam, on the outskirts of Sultan Hussein's walled enclosure. The Malays were the next most numerous Muslim community, and the Arab traders followed them. Each community built places of worship, at times quite distinct from one another.

The Masjid Al-Abrar, the Nagore Durgha in Telok Ayer Street, and the Jamae Mosque (or Chulia Mosque) in South Bridge Road, are all three of a type. They are squared enclosures partly

Nagore Durgha, Telok Ayer Street. 1820–30, (top)

Masjid Al-Abrar, Telok Ayer Street. 1850–55, (bottom left)

Masjid Jamae (Chulia Mosque), South Bridge Road, 1830, (bottom right)

Masjid Hajjah Fatimah, Beach Road,
1845-46

roofed, and surrounded by a brick wall
with two minarets at either front corner.
They are all quite small structures, almost
humble, but have still managed through
decoration to retain their individuality.
The Al-Abrar mosque, built in 1850-55,
known also as *Kuchu Palli* in Tamil (Hut
Mosque), is the simplest with its plain
single banded miniature minarets, topped
by fat, onion-shaped *chatri* (dome). The
chatri are echoed along the facade above
the latticed balustrade.

The Chulia or Jamae mosque at South
Bridge Road, built in 1830, is slightly
more detailed. With a simple rusticated
base, supporting two stepped and
window-pierced minarets, it is still extremely simple, but hints at the Islamic
love of intricate pierced abstract
decoration.

The Nagore Durgha Shrine, further
along Telok Ayer Street, is more ornate,
and curiously combines a classical street
level facade with, above it, a pierced
Islamic balustrade with two stepped
minarets. The fluted Corinthian pillars
and half moon fan lights above the doors
could almost be part of a separate building, as they have little in common with the
intricate work above them. The shrine
was built in 1828-30.

The mosque in Beach Road, for the
Malay-Arab community, is much grander, and better built. Called the Masjid
Hajjah Fatimah, after the Malaccan lady
who commissioned the building in
1845-46, the building displays a hybrid of
architectural styles. In the traditional
way, it is a squared walled enclosure, with
a domed main prayer hall, a bathing area
for the ritual washing, and a school. The
central minaret, and the two flanking
houses, are European in style, although
the houses display many Chinese features
in the shape of the windows and the
surrounding woodwork.

It has been suggested that the minaret

Sri Mariamman Temple, South Bridge Road, 1842-43

was built by J. T. Thomson, the architect of the first St. Andrews' spire, and that the two are similar, which is not the case. The minaret has two octagonal towers, the upper one smaller, and resting inside the balustrade of the lower. Each corner of the octagon has one rounded and two flat Doric pilasters. The windows at ground level and in the two towers are circular and heavily moulded, resembling portholes, and the dentilation on the cornice is also moulded in deep relief. The mosque was designed by an unknown British architect, and then left in the hands of French contractors, who used Malay labour for the construction work. It has inherited therefore, a unique universal flavour.

The structure and style of the principal Hindu temples in early Singapore are those of Southern India and Ceylon, for most of the original Indian settlers were

Tamils from the South, among them architects, craftsmen and builders. The earliest temple of Sri Mariamman in South Bridge Road, like many of the other mosques, churches, and temples, was a wood and attap one built in the 1820's after the owner of the plot, Naraina Pillai, of the brickworks fame, obtained authorization to build a temple. The present temple was built in 1842-43, with Indian convict labour, but has since been extensively restored and embellished.

The temple is dedicated to Devi, the most universal of the Hindu divinities, and considered the Mother Goddess. Three principal elements characterize Southern Indian Hindu temples: the shrine, or altar, and there may be many, is identified by a decorated dome, or *vimanam*. In Sri Mariamman, the *vimanam* are onion shaped and textured like pineapples. The *madapam*, or hall, is the main assembly room, and often comprises a nave flanked with columns. It

Vimanam, Sri Mariammmam Temple

can, however, be left as an open square in front of the main shrine.

Of great significance in Southern Indian temples is the entrance tower, or *gopuram,* and every temple has one. It acts in the same way as a Christian church spire does, and identifies the temple from afar for pilgrims, who can then start offering prayers while approaching the temple. The Sri Mariamman temple has a *gopuram* with six levels. It is shaped like a rectangular pyramid, and like all *gopuram,* is covered in a profusion of statuary. The sculpture on Sri Mariamman is relatively recent and dates from 1932-35. Like the Chinese, the Hindus have a love of richly carved figurative decoration, which is often extremely realistic, and highly coloured. The pantheon of Hindu deities sits around the *vimanam* and on the *gopuram* in relaxed natural poses.

The floral and abstract decoration elsewhere in the temple is in deep relief, and like the other arts from Southern India, such as their music and dance, is vigorous and bold. The relief carving was designed to be viewed in the strong sun, unlike some European classical mouldings which do not travel well from the weak northern light, and which flatten and lose themselves in tropical sunlight.

Lamentably, the last of the needs of the population to be considered were facilities for the sick, for when it came to servicing the medical needs of the community, the East India Company were extremely loathe to part with funds. The early Europeans were remarkably healthy, and existed on the services of a few private practitioners. The Straits Times of 1861 declared "We are the healthiest community in the East.....", and very few Europeans, except for visiting infected sailors, or women and small children, are found in the Christian graveyards, as the vast majority survived to see retirement.

The story differed though, in the

Tan Tock Seng Hospital, Pearl's Hill.
J.T. Thomson, 1844

densely populated areas, where sanitation was poor, opium smoking rife, and malnutrition a common ailment. Sailors, too, were victims of poor health, as stranded in Singapore for months on end, with fluctuating prospects of work and little money, they were easy prey for diseases. In the end it was left to private individuals to provide the money, for both a Paupers' hospital, and a Seaman's hospital. Tan Tock Seng put up the bulk of the funds needed for the Paupers' hospital, and it was appropriately named after him. The foundation stones for both the hospitals, to be built side by side at the base of Pearls Hill, was laid in 1844, and the architect was designated to be the Government Surveyor to the Colony, J.T. Thomson. Like Jackson's Singapore Institution, the two hospitals are severely classical, with an imposing facade of columns rising the height of the buildings.

For all its classical splendour, and the Press description of "handsome edifices adding much to the appearance of the town", the two hospitals were badly sited right in front of a large marshy swamp (Balestier Plain) which did nothing to improve the health of the patients. In 1857 after the Indian Mutiny, the buildings were taken over for military purposes, and the hospitals transferred to more congenial and healthy surroundings.

Another building which was designed to service the community, and which is still very much in action today, is St. Joseph's Institution. It was founded by the French Catholic priest Father Beurel, who had arrived in Singapore in 1837 with the dream of starting schools for both girls and boys of all races and religions. In 1852 he brought out six Catholic brothers from France, one of whom, Brother Lothaire, was responsible for designing the central section of the boys' school in 1865. The school was built on the site of the first Catholic church in Singapore

Seaman's Hospital, Pearl's Hill.
J.T. Thomson, 1844, (top)

St. Joseph's Institution, Bras Basah.
Brother Lothaire, 1865. Wings added by
Father Nain, 1900, (bottom)

St. Joseph's Institution, Bras Basah.
Brother Lothaire, 1865

along Bras Basah Road, which was closed after the Cathedral of the Good Shepherd was completed in 1846. It is a charming building, quite ornate, with early Christian arches, and decorative plasterwork. On two storeys, it has a central arched carriage porch, and a rounded dome rising from the centre of the roof. The radiating wings were added much later in 1900, in the same style, and were again designed by one of the priests, Father Nain. He also built the chapel and gymnasium behind the building slightly later in 1911-12. Father Beurel's girls' school, as was mentioned previously, opened in 1854, in Mr Caldwell's house just across the street.

Not all Singapore's early buildings were fortunate in having as architects such gifted and sensitively trained amateurs as Brother Lothaire. One unlucky amateur, Captain Faber, the Superintendent of the Madras Engineers in the 1840's, had severe problems with his building projects. He built a bridge over the Singapore River so low that the lighters (*tonkangs*) could not pass under it at high tide, and was amazed at the negative response to his suggestion that the river directly under the bridge should be dredged to lower the water level. In 1846 the roof of the "covered landing place ..... at the front of the Government Offices ..... gave way and seriously injured several workmen. The pillars were too thin and the roof came down with a rush". Faber did, however, manage to do a few things right, and we can thank him today for his road up Mount Faber, although it is slightly narrow, and the Gothic archway entrances to Fort Canning Park.

By the 1840's the first Chinatown houses were showing signs of age, and in 1844 the houses of merchants in Telok Ayer Street, Pekin Street, Market Street, Circular Road, and Boat Quay were deemed a "public nuisance by the reason of the very decayed and unsafe condition of the said several houses or buildings". The owners were ordered to pull them down within three months and build better ones. In stages such as this Chinatown was rebuilt with successively more sophisticated building materials and designs, although they retained right up to the end of the century that distinctive and very simple Chinese shophouse style.

A new standard of office and shop architecture was initiated with the erection of the Ellenborough Building. Commissioned by Tan Tock Seng, and designed by J. T. Thomson in 1845, it was one of the first conscious attempts in Singapore to build a unified row of shops, which not only afforded practicality, but also aimed at a certain aesthetic standard of architecture. This was followed up in 1864 by the completion of the land reclamation from Fort Fullerton to Telok Ayer, and the building of Collyer Quay. Supported by a strong sea wall, the row of offices and shops that were built along the Quay in a Neo-Renaissance style, and which were "one of the sights of the Far East", set a new tone in commercial architecture, and paved the way for the splendid array of offices that were to be built later in the century.

Ellenborough Building, Ellenborough Street. J.T. Thomson, 1845, (top)

Collyer Quay in 1900, (bottom)

ECLECTIC EXPANSION
1880 — 1900

Until the 1860's Singapore had remained very much the same size as in the 1840's, the town plans showing the same basic layout of the streets. In the 1880's expansion took place in all directions: West out towards the New Harbour (later renamed Keppel Harbour after Sir Henry Keppel); North from the river along River Valley Road, up Orchard Road towards Tanglin's emerging residential area; up Serangoon Road, with continual building over the old market gardens, towards the far side of the island; Eastwards towards Geylang and Katong.

Between 1880 and 1900 there was an enormous increase in the population. 150,000 Chinese immigrants had flooded the shores of Singapore in the unsettled last days of the Ching Dynasty. Word of the boom in prosperity in Singapore would have reached their ears: Singapore was riding high on the wave of increased trade between Europe and the Far East, an increase of eight times between 1873 and 1913. The commercial viability of steamships reduced the sailing time from months to weeks, and the opening of the Suez Canal had shortened the trip still further. Now regular postal communications put commercial transactions on a more reliable footing. Many more women and families joined the community of European bachelors and changed society in Singapore from the swashbuckling adventurer's life to one of more organized

sedateness. Some remarked that the romance went out of life in Singapore when the ladies arrived.

The town was reaching a size now where life really had to be more organized and institutionalized. In 1884 the submission of all building plans to the government authorities was made compulsory and building thus more controlled. The Public Works Department had been set up in 1873. Measures such as these reflect a much increased civic awareness, very different from the days when there were no taxes and the residents would not vote enough public money to maintain such basic amenities as a police force or town cleaning service.

Few of the shophouses of this era still stand, but contemporary plans and elevations for a row of shophouses in Serangoon Road give a good clue to the physical development of the town. In the plans that were submitted for houses, both detached and terraced, for stabling, animal pens and slaughter houses, we can establish the nature of this area as one of the centres of the butcher trade and a centre of buffalo cart goods transport. Certainly "Little India" is a microcosm of the cosmopolitan atmosphere that was typical of Singapore. Although Raffles had divided the town into separate racial areas, where commerce or special interests were concerned, the races mixed freely. For instance, the race track was built on one side of the Serangoon Road area. It

Map of the Town of Singapore
by J.C. Woods, 1881

resulted in a number of Europeans living in this part of the predominantly Indian community. Plans were also submitted by Chinese and Malay speculators for terraced housing. The grand drawings for the row of shophouses in Serangoon Road itself can be matched to the actual buildings still standing in the street.

On the edge of "Little India" in Ophir Road a church was built in 1888 with funds collected by members of the Indian community who came from Pondicherry. Named Our Lady of Lourdes, the little church survives today in good condition. Gothic in character, there are some curious anomalies in the design. The main doors to the West end are similar to those found in a godown. The exterior walls are supported by buttresses. In the interior instead of a chancel the nave is rounded at the altar end, and aisles extend in an arc round the church. The interior feels light and open because the columns in the colonnade are made of cast iron, and therefore much slimmer than masonry. They were constructed by Izambert of Paris and shipped to Singapore. The nave rises to a clerestory above, flooding the church with natural light. In the place of the conventional altar Our Lady of Lourdes has a small replica of the grotto of Lourdes with the Virgin Mary standing in it. A remarkable crucifix with outstretched arms hangs on the wall near the altar, and legend relates that when thieves once tried to wrest it from its place it refused to move. The modern stained glass and the bells were installed in the 1950's with the aid of a subscription from the congregation. At the back of the church in one corner a splendid wrought iron spiral staircase gives access to the choir stalls and the organ. This church is active today, with charismatic prayer meetings every Friday evening at which faith healing sessions take place.

The bulk of the Chinese population

Plan of Shophouses, Serangoon Road, 1891,
(top)

Shophouses, Serangoon Road. 1891,
(bottom)

Terraced House, Telok Ayer Street, c. 1900

lived in Chinatown, with the more well-to-do residents and Straits Chinese living in the area around Telok Ayer Street and Amoy Street. Some three storey houses still survive in this area. The typical house favoured by the Straits Chinese consisted of a front room the width of the plot with a second room behind it. A more luxurious house might have another room behind that. In one corner of the second or third room rose the staircase to the floors above. Behind these rooms the ground floor was divided lengthways into a kitchen and storage area. The rear wall of the kitchen was often left at half height, open to the elements, with an overhang and a high wall behind it so that maximum ventilation was available while privacy and shelter were retained.

The expansion of Singapore meant yet more wealth for some and a growth in the number of large houses. A small number of wealthy Chinese merchants or *towkays* built their houses on the traditional Chinese plan. Four such houses were built around this time. Tan Seng Pok finished his house in Hill Street in 1869. This ultimately became the Chinese Consulate before it was pulled down. The last of the four to be built, that belonging to Tan Yeok Nee in Tank Road, was constructed in 1885 and still survives today. Distinctive Chinese roofs and curved eaves easily identify it, although much of the former garden has been lost to road widening projects. Inside, the individual halls are completely open, fronting onto the courtyards. Spectacularly carved mythical beasts decorate the roof brackets and there are corbels made of ornamental plaster, their cream colour contrasting with the dark stained beams. The stone carvings and massive granite piers are believed to have been imported from China. The survival of the house is something of a miracle, as it has had a chequered history. When the railway was laid through Tank Road, the noise and dust drove the Tan family away and the house was sold to the Railway as the official residence of the Station Master. The next change came in 1919 when the Malayan Railway was centralized in Kuala Lumpur and the government handed over the house in the form of a trust to the Anglican Bishop of Singapore, Bishop Ferguson-Davis. For the next twenty years it served as St. Mary's Home and School for Girls. Then in 1940, just before Singapore became involved in the Second World War, the Salvation Army bought the house. Between 1942-45 the Japanese army took it over, inflicting considerable damage. After the war the Salvation Army regained possession and spent a large sum of money on reconditioning the house. They continue to occupy it today as their administrative headquarters. It has been designated a national monument and remains a familiar sight in Singapore.

More people, more wealth, meant more temples. Luckily there were several Chinese temples built in this period which still stand today. One outstanding example is the Giok Hong Tian temple in Havelock Road. Geomancy is very important to all Chinese buildings and this temple was felt to be in a fortunate geomantic position. As described in a Chinese inscription on the Giok Hong Tian plaque dated 1887, it was built in a "peaceful and wholesome street" with the hill at its back and the Singapore River in front. Surrounded by greenery the site was clearly a good choice. It is unfortunate that a noisy five lane arterial road now runs close to the temple's side and that tall HDB flats and nondescript small business complexes cut it off from the river. However, its flowing ornamental roofs and three pavilions can still be seen easily from the street. Wild dancing dragons flank the magical celestial blazing

Our Lady of Lourdes, Ophir Road, 1888

Tan Yeok Nee House (Salvation Army),
Tank Road. 1885, (top)

Interior, Tan Yeok Nee House, Tank Road.
1885, (bottom left)

Roof detail, Giok Hong Tian Temple,
Havelock Road. 1887, (top right)

Thong Chai Medical Institution, Wayang
Street. 1892, (bottom right)

pearl on the roof ridge. The ridge is decorated further with colourful ceramic flowers, plants and birds of good omen. The roof hips are terminated by statues of the Gods of Sun, Rain, Winds and Thunder, whose presence wards off dangers and evil influences. The ridge over the entrance has interesting fish dragons, symbols of success and achievement.

In this fast developing period, as the soul, so the body was catered for. In 1892 the Thong Chai medical institution was built in Wayang Street in the Chinese style, with money raised from a public subscription. Its triple curved ornamental gables remain the most graceful in Singapore. The three gables indicate the three halls. These in turn are separated from each other by two open courtyards. The roof of the second hall is of great height with splendid tall posts and long beams exposing the traditional Chinese method of roof construction. The posts and purlins support a roof covered with Chinese tiles. In the second courtyard a green glazed ceramic balustrade encircles the second storey. These earthenware balusters are locally made and can be seen in many dwellings in Singapore.

At the same time as these buildings were being erected by the expanding citizenry, public buildings of many types were also being commissioned by the colonial authorities. In 1882 the first Singapore General Hospital was created at Kandang Kerbau. In 1891 the second Ellenborough market was built near Read Bridge. The market became the centre of the fish trade in New Bridge Road. In 1899 it was extended when a wrought iron pavilion at the Edinburgh Exhibition was

Roof detail, Telok Ayer Market, Robinson Road. J. MacRitchie, 1894, (top)

Telok Ayer Market, Robinson Road. J. MacRitchie, 1894, (bottom)

dismantled, shipped to Singapore and re-assembled there.

After the reclamation of Telok Ayer Basin plans were laid for a new expanded central market in an extended Market Street. The municipal engineer, James MacRitchie (immortalized by the reservoir that bears his name), designed the new market and it was ready for business on March 1st, 1894. He planned one main market with a fish market next door, sensibly overhanging the sea. Due to continual subsidence and problems with the foundations, the fish market was considerably delayed. For the main structure MacRitchie devised a building octagonal in shape, to be constructed of wrought iron with a slate roof.

The contract for supplying the iron went to the firm of P & W McLellan of Glasgow. MacRitchie's design followed the basic shape of Coleman's for the earlier market that this replaced. His use of iron filigree decoration lends a light and airy atmosphere to the market both inside and on the roof, where an open dome of iron perches above a small elegant clock tower. It has been claimed that the antecedent for the open dome was a church in Glasgow. The use of iron for construction and ornamentation, and the distinctive shape create a very successful building. Gazetted a national monument in 1973, it is now no longer a market but a food centre.

With an expanding and more mobile community, several new bridges were built upstream over the Singapore River. New Bridge Road was connected to Hill Street by the New Bridge (alias Coleman Bridge) in 1886, a structure as elegant in its own way as Coleman's own architecture. The railings along the sides are of ornamental ironwork and the graceful shallow curves of the substructure make it one of the most attractive of the seven bridges spanning the river. From the pontoons in the water octagonal piers

*New Bridge (Coleman Bridge), Hill Street to
New Bridge Road. 1886, (top)*

*Cavanagh Bridge.
1890, (bottom)*

painted white and brown hold up the bridge and on top of these rise graceful wrought iron gas lamps on standards. The elegance of this bridge is in marked contrast to the contemporary Read Bridge (named after a prominent businessman, W. H. M. Read), which has little to elevate it above its utilitarian basics. Built in 1889 Read Bridge replaced the Merchant Bridge which, as has been mentioned, was designed by the unfortunate Captain Faber and was too low for the *tongkangs* or lighters to pass under at high tide.

The last two buildings and the new bridges (the Cavenagh Bridge had been constructed in 1890) reveal an awareness in Singapore of one of the most exciting building materials to emerge in the 19th Century. Throughout the second half of the century, the most modern buildings in England, such as the Great Exhibition building of 1851 and many railway stations, were constructed of iron. This new material was light and strong and could be manufactured in a factory. It was ideally suited to the industrial revolution and the new awareness it generated. Until this time it would have been unthinkable to dismantle a building, ship it half way across the world, and reassemble it.

Many further good works were undertaken in this period and institutions were founded. The most important institution to be established in the 1880's was Raffles Museum and Library, built to house natural history collections and ethnological specimens, as well as a national library. In May 1882 plans had been submitted by the Colonial Engineer, Major McCallum of the Public Works Department, and after delayed approval by the colonial authorities, work had started in 1884. The erection of the dome had proved too much for the first contractor, the task literally driving him mad. The second contractor happily retained his sanity to completion and the building was finished in 1887 at the cost of a mere $80,000, nicely under the original estimate of $83,530. In his speech commemorating the opening of the Museum, Governor Weld quoted from his original proposal made in 1882, which reflects the state of establishment Singapore had achieved: "I hope that you will agree with me in thinking that the Museum and Library should be on a scale commensurate with the growing importance of the Colony." The result of such sentiments was a building whose frontage measures 240 feet and whose dome rises 90 feet above the main building, itself 50 feet in height. The layout of the building consists of two broad wings of equal length flanking a central rotunda capped by a silver dome. The outside of the building is plastered and was originally coloured to represent freestone: "The number of windows painted chocolate and red and the ornamentation give sufficient variety." The entrance to the building is covered by a wide portico which gives onto a short passage into the open rotunda. The eye is immediately led upwards to the dome by the straight vertical lines of the giant engaged columns, rising through two floors. Niches in the ground floor walls of the rotunda were designed to hold statues symbolic of the Sciences and the Arts. The other openings on the ground floor lead to the wings. In the right wing on the ground floor was housed the Library, with bookshelves projecting from the spaces between the double rows of windows. Proper attention was paid to ventilation so that the room would not smell musty, a familiar Singapore problem at the time. On the opposite side were small specimen rooms, meeting rooms and offices. The upstairs is reached by an elegant staircase. This leads to the gallery around the dome in which was housed the ethnological collection, the room over the porch housing the minerological and shell collections, with specimens from the Malay Peninsula. In

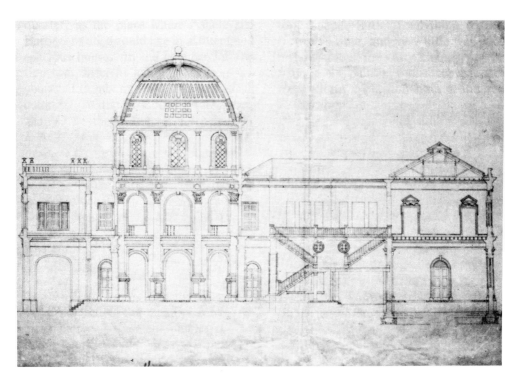

Sectional drawing, Raffles Museum and Library, Stamford Road. Major McCallum, 1884–87, (top)

Raffles Museum and Library (National Museum and Art Gallery), Stamford Road. Major McCallum, 1884–87, (bottom)

Third pavilion, Singapore Cricket Club, the Padang. 1884

the right wing over the Library was the Zoological collection. This room was lit by lantern lights set into the roof. Beyond this gallery was another for Botanical specimens. In the corresponding left wing the exhibits from the Arts and Manufactures were to be housed. Beyond that lay the Curator's quarters.

This building remained adequate for the Museum collections and library for only two years, for then enquiries were made as to whether Fort Canning House could be made available for the Curator. This eventually happened and his offices were turned into galleries. When space became really pressing an extension was built at the back of the site, forming an H to the main building. A bridge on the upper level connected the two. This took three years to build and was opened in 1907. Next, an extension for the Library was planned, and was added to the Tanglin end of the extension block. Its completion was delayed until 1918 because of the Second World War. The library remained there until 1953 when its

own building was completed next door. The Natural history collections were moved to the Science Centre in Jurong when it opened in 1974. Now the National Museum concentrates its efforts on the arts and ethnological collections. Expansions and renovations have continued throughout its existence and in 1984 included a complete interior rearrangement and remodelling.

Private sector institutional buildings were also coming up. The Tanglin and Teutonic Clubs had already been founded in the 1860's and an embryonic Cricket Club was already in existence. The latter's clubhouse, erected in 1877, was certainly better than the very temporary shelter which served the cricketers between 1859 and 1870, but remained little more than a square hut in which to keep the bats and the beer. In 1884 a third clubhouse was built on a cast iron frame with verandahs all round. It was on two levels, the upper level being the ladies' viewing gallery. On the cast iron columns under the balconies, floral capitals surmount the columns and act as a base for the splendid floral brackets which support the roof. All of these can still be seen today. At this time, how-

79

Raffles Hotel, Beach Road. R.A.J. Bidwell, 1899

ever, the balconies continued all around this building. The further extensions which were added later are described in the next chapter.

The number of travellers to Singapore also increased steadily, and the largest hotel to date was founded at this time. The Sarkies brothers, Armenians of long standing in the Straits Settlements, took over Dane's Tiffin Rooms on Beach Road and — with the house next door — established Raffles Hotel in 1885. The core of the hotel, as we know it, was built in 1899, one of the grandest in South East Asia at the time, on a par with the Eastern and Oriental Hotel in Penang and the Strand Hotel in Rangoon. Indeed, there are certain features which are common to the Strand and Raffles. The central Bar and Tiffin Room are built as an open court with a roof skylight over the top, rising through the building so that the

entrances to the rooms on the intervening levels are from the balconies looking down over the restaurant. The Raffles Hotel had a gracious Palm Court and a grand entrance way in the middle of the Beach Road facade. The two ends of the facade broke forward at an angle framing the entrance way and carriage circle. Later, when the ballroom was added, the entrance was sadly moved to the corner of one of these wings and makes for a less imposing arrival. The hotel has had a colourful history, amusingly described in Ilsa Sharp's book *There is Only One Raffles*. Many famous characters have stayed there, or at least had a drink in the long bar. Somerset Maugham is said to have written *Of Human Bondage* and *The Moon and Sixpence* in the Hotel and Noel Coward was there too. Unfortunately, later additions have marred the stately, balanced look of the Hotel, but renovations are planned in an effort to restore her to her former glory. The exterior of the building is uncomplicated, with some

Hongkong and Shanghai Banking Corpn,
Collyer Quay. Swan and Maclaren.
1892, (top)

Chartered Bank Building, Battery Road.
1895, (bottom)

nice decorative plasterwork and facades. Significantly, the Hotel was one of the first of the numerous projects of R. A. J. Bidwell of Swan and MacLaren, the architectural firm of which much more will be heard.

All this expansion was founded on Singapore's growing success as a place of trade and business, and the two decades saw a bustle of activity in the development of commercial buildings. One of the biggest was the Hong Kong and Shanghai Banking Corporation building, completed in 1892 and aptly described as a "wedding cake". It is ascribed to the firm of Swan and MacLaren. The overall impression is of a grand mass of detail, a multiplicity of gables soaring over the polychrome stonework of the facade. The closest analogy may well be the work of Norman Shaw, at that time building such London landmarks as the New Scotland Yard Building and the red brick houses with ornamental gables in Chelsea, nicknamed "Pont Street Dutch". It must have created a rather extravagant impression alongside the older buildings on Collyer Quay, lower in height, with their elegant balconies and uniform facades. The history of building in Singapore has always been one of the big jolt, a major change of scale in size, height or grandness of buildings heralding a new architectural period. This building signalled such a change in the early 1900's. Its prominent position in Battery Road made the building a landmark in Singapore, and important dignitaries landing at Johnstone's Pier saw it as the gateway to Singapore. The building itself lasted only until 1919 when it was demolished to make way for a more modern and larger successor.

The contrast between the Hong Kong Bank design and the style of the Chartered Bank Building, erected in 1895 on the corner of Flint Street and Battery Road, demonstrates the freedom that architects had to design in any style they wished. This was a gracious and balanced building, with its rusticated podium and alternating pilasters and columns on the facade, rounded off by an entablature and balustrade on which stood a series of urns. Apart from the rather eccentric window designs, this could have been one of the most classic of late 19th Century buildings in Singapore. Unfortunately by 1905 the bank had outgrown the building and moved out. The building was eventually pulled down in the 1930's.

By the end of the 19th Century the commercial centre of Singapore had a number of appropriately stately office buildings of which any European city would have been proud. Most of these buildings have remained anonymous, but some are worth mentioning. Number two Finlayson Green, which housed insurance and shipping companies, was as pure an example of Renaissance revival as could be found in the Far East. Its triple tiered colonnade was fronted with single and double free standing columns lending dignity to the facade. On each tier, an entablature appropriate to it corresponded to each classical order. The ends of the building projected slightly forward and were more ornately detailed, finished off at the roof by segmental pediments. The impression given to the viewer was one of harmony and good proportion.

For the most part idiosyncratic flamboyance was the ruling architectural style of the period. For instance, the fanciful and ornate Bonham Building dominated Bonham Street for many years. Many buildings which stood on corner sites took advantage of their prominent positions to display architectural variety, by adding a contrasting arch or a projecting lantern at the roof. Two such examples were the Netherlands Trading Society at the corner of Cecil and d'Almeida Streets, and the Boustead Institution in Tanjong Pagar, built in 1892 with funds donated by

*Netherlands Trading Society, Cecil Street.
c. 1890, (top)*

*South over Finlayson Green in 1890,
(bottom)*

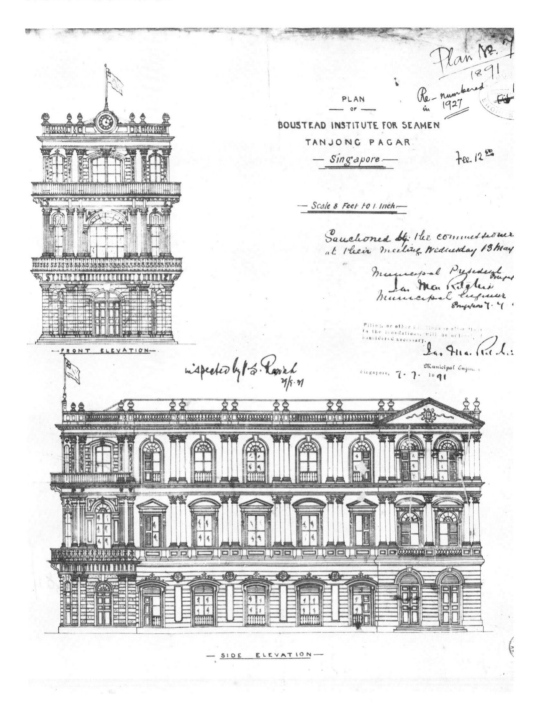

PLAN
OF
BOUSTEAD INSTITUTE FOR SEAMEN
TANJONG PAGAR
— Singapore —

Plan N°. 7
1891
Re-numbered
in 1927

Fee 12.

— Scale 8 Feet to 1 Inch —

— FRONT ELEVATION —

— SIDE ELEVATION —

Boustead Institute for Seamen, Tanjong Pagar. 1892, (above and top right)

Police Court, South Bridge Road. c. 1890, (bottom right)

The Police Court, Singapore.

Edward Boustead for the establishment of a hostel for merchant seamen.

The businessmen needed other facilities besides their stately office buildings and at this time Singapore was also rapidly developing its transportation system. The Tanjong Pagar Dock Company consolidated itself from four dock companies in the 1880's and the Singapore Tramway Company laid track along the coast between its premises and the centre of the town. This relieved some of the congestion on the roads and made life more secure for those trying to negotiate the lawless, frightening traffic of Singapore. The Tanjong Pagar Company, later the Port of Singapore Authority, was also the first to build housing for its workers.

One last word on utilities: on the 19th of May 1882 a fountain was unveiled to the memory of Tan Kim Seng whose gene-rosity had made possible the transport of fresh water from Peninsular Malaya to Singapore. The fountain, "a handsome, showy iron structure, ... was made by Andrew Handyside and Co Ltd of Derby and London, and was erected on its present site in the square facing the Exchange Building". Today it stands on the esplanade, a familiar sight to all Singaporeans.

Thus the building in the 1880's and 1890's was considerable, and the styles various. Indeed, some splendidly eclectic buildings were erected as public institutions: the Police Court in South Bridge Road happily combined a Malay porch and a French inspired mansard roof. Across the road the Central Police Station built in 1882 was a more ornate version of Raffles Institution, with a very individual interpretation of a Baroque-Islamic clock tower. Nevertheless, in these years there would have been no mistake that Singapore took great pride in itself, in its prosperity and its growing institutions.

Police Headquarters, South Bridge Road.
1882

THE BOOM TOWN
1900 — 1920

Around the turn of the century two things happened that ensured the wealth of the Malay States, and of Singapore as their principal commercial outlet and port. Henry Ford made the automobile a viable proposition with his Model T Ford. Each car had four wheels plus a spare, which needed tyres made of rubber. At about the same time a process was developed for canning food using tin. With these two events the fortunes of the Straits Tin Company were secured and the rubber industry was launched. This was timely; the coffee crop had failed in 1897 and the plantation owners were keen to find something else to replace it with. From his laboratory in the Gardens at Holland Road and Cluny Road, Henry Ridley, Director of the Botanic Gardens from 1888-1912, developed a foolproof way of tapping rubber trees without hampering their growth. Those men with the courage and sense to listen to him made fortunes and by the 1920's Malaya was supplying half the world's rubber.

The effect on Singapore was dramatic: by 1903 Singapore was the world's seventh largest port in terms of shipping tonnage. The facilities offered, however, remained grossly inadequate, cramped and congested. As a result of disorganization in the early years of the 20th Century squabbles between vested interests and lack of modern equipment were continuing problems. Ox-carts still transported all goods to and from the docks. The need for improvements was pressing, and when the board of the Tanjong Pagar Dock Company refused to sanction improvements which would cost $12 million the Government nationalized the company, making it into the Tanjong Pagar Dock Board. Between 1905 and 1910 the dock and port facilities were modernized: old wharves were replaced; new roads and godowns were built; modern machinery was installed. The reclaimed Telok Ayer Basin was developed, a wet dock was constructed and electric power was introduced. The graving dock, the second largest in the world, was completed in 1913 and the giant Empire Dock finished in 1917. The modernization of the port came just in time to cope with rapid opening of the interior amid spiralling world demand for rubber and tin.

These changes really signalled an important rise in Singapore's stature in the international business world. Physically Singapore was already beginning to look like a formal outpost of the British Empire, with a full variety of European buildings. This process continued in the first years of the 20th Century.

Much of this development was accounted for by the architectural firm of Swan and MacLaren, which was to build substantial buildings in a great variety of national and religious styles. The Raffles Hotel of 1899 has already been mentioned. They were also commissioned to rebuild the Teutonia Club in 1901 in its

Teutonia Club, Scotts Road. R.A.J. Bidwell, Swan and MacLaren, 1901

new location in Scotts Road, after it moved from its original position behind Raffles Hotel in North Bridge Road. In 1905 came the extensions and rebuilding of the Victoria Memorial Hall in the same year as the Chassed El Synagogue in Oxley Rise. 1907 saw the extension and transformation of the Cricket Club as well as the construction of Telephone House in Robinson Road. Between 1906 and 1912 Swan and MacLaren rebuilt the church of St. Joseph in Victoria Street dedicated to our Lady of Fatimah. They also designed and built one of the largest shops in early Singapore, John Little's department store in Raffles Place, located on the opposite side of the square from Robinson and Company. One of the last of this group of buildings was a large villa for the Chinese businessman, Eu Tong Sen, erected on Mount Sophia.

Such was their importance to this period that a brief history of the firm of Swan and MacLaren and its leading architect at that time, R. A. J. Bidwell, is in order. Two surveyor engineers called Swan and Lermit had first established their architectural practice in 1887. After three years Lermit withdrew and J. W. B. MacLaren, another surveyor engineer, replaced him. In 1892 the firm became known as Swan and MacLaren and continues to practise today under that name. Regent Alfred John Bidwell joined the firm in 1895 arriving in Singapore from England by way of a short working stay in the Public Works Department in Kuala Lumpur. He was the first professionally trained architect in Singapore since Coleman had practised in the town in the 1820's and 30's. Here he surely found a fabulous opportunity to exercise all his knowledge of the full range and variety of Western architectural vocabulary.

After a fairly conventional but well planned Raffles Hotel, he branched into

*Victoria Memorial Hall and Theatre,
Empress Place. R.A.J. Bidwell, Swan and
MacLaren, 1905*

the south German style for the Teutonic
Club. Typical of this regional style is the
use of pastel colour on ornamental relief
work contrasting with white facings, as
are the large semicircular gable ends
flanking the entrance. These features are
enhanced by the dramatic possibilities of
the sloping site. The whole of this inspired
arrangement is topped by an octagonal
tower and pointed tiled roof, again taken
from the German vernacular. It is fortunate that these features were retained
when the Club was adapted to a hotel
after the First World War. Notable are
the rustications on the windows, as these
became a hallmark of Bidwell's work.

The more classical Victoria Memorial
Hall incorporated and enlarged the Victoria Theatre which had been built in 1862
by the Municipal Engineer, John Bennett.
The original building still remains but it

was refaced by Bidwell to harmonize with
the hall next door in 1905. Each building
is marked by its own giant portico with
generous columns rising up to triangular
pediments, and standing firmly on a
heavy rusticated base. As a finishing
touch to the parapet an elegant balustrade
augments the roofline, interrupted by
alternated pediments, triangular on the
entrances, segmental in the centre and the
ends. Some interesting architectural features are used on the walls, the most prominent being the bay window in the centre
of the facade. Between double pilasters it
breaks forward in a concave curve, its
three windows separated by ornamental
rustication on the piers. The segmental
pediment on the roof is echoed by a
smaller version over the bay window. This
is one of the many distorted Mannerist
features which ornament the building,
others being the oriole windows on the
third storey and the attic colonnade of
rusticated disengaged columns under the
roof at the ends of the building. The side

89

Chassed EL Synagogue, Oxley Rise.
R.A.J. Bidwell, Swan and MacLaren,
1905, (top)

Singapore Cricket Club, the Padang.
R.A.J. Bidwell, Swan and MacLaren,
1907, (bottom)

elevations would have a greater three dimensional impact had they not been filled in when the building was modernized and airconditioning installed. The interior planning has been maintained, the large halls upstairs retaining their original proportions and the majority of their original decoration, an example being the dignified arches displaying very prominent keystones in the concert hall. The clocktower on the Victoria Memorial Hall was a landmark in the days before its eclipse by high rise buildings. It has banded stucco with some intricate geometry around the clock, emphasizing curve and square below a black cupola supported by scrolls. As a whole, the building suggests a playful sort of classical revival.

In the same year the firm had a chance to try out classical architecture with a different flavour in a commission to build a private synagogue in Oxley Rise for the wealthy Jewish businessman, Menasseh Meyer. Here Bidwell's inspiration is the Byzantine church, both in the plan, consisting of a wide nave and high aisles, and in the details. A single wide arch spans the apse and this is supported on composite corbels which give it a Byzantine flavour. The Byzantine theme is further expressed in the clustered columns in the nave. A large imposing porch and narthex house the stairs which rise to the galleries above. In a synagogue, as in a mosque, women must worship separately in the gallery as it is feared they will distract men's minds from concentrating on the tora. The galleries are ornamented by delicate ironwork into whose design is woven Meyer's initials. An extremely attractive arrangement of the windows with triple fan lights shows the originality of Bidwell's fertile mind. On the exterior, the synagogue is heavily rusticated, with "stones" in plasterwork, alternating rough and smooth. Out of a relatively uncomplicated ground plan he created a stimulating and harmonious whole.

In the following year the Cricket Club was given extensions to its square central core. Instead of expanding the club straight out along the end of the Padang, Bidwell framed the cricket pitch by dividing the extensions into two sections projecting at angles to the main clubhouse. This gave the mass more variety of form and provided even greater opportunity to indulge in the creative disposition of windows, and in decorative plasterwork. The flavour here is that of the English country house, with large Elizabethan multipaned windows below a substantial pediment in which his favourite oriole window retains the central position. He also had an opportunity to create alternating triangular and segmental pediments by dividing up the whole into three sections. His sense of three dimensional massing was assured, for the additional jack roof above the main roof saves the whole from being a horizontal bore. The viewing galleries were extended along the wings and the wrought iron columns with their handsome floral brackets were continued from the side balconies of the old clubhouse into the new ones. The only unpoetic note is the very heavy entrance portico, which was originally red brick and white plaster; perhaps the intention was for this haven of relaxation to present a ponderous face to the public. There is even a local feature in the garden front where a typical Malay splayed staircase has been used to approach the central section of the balcony. Its curved lines aptly round off a very successful building.

The next year, 1907, saw the completion of the Telephone House in Robinson Road. Its neighbour, the Telok Ayer Food Centre (formerly market) is a preserved national monument, and it is hoped that the Telephone House will receive the same distinction as the last survivor of the old scale in this part of central Singapore. The impression this building

Telephone House, Robinson Road. R.A.J. Bidwell, Swan and MacLaren, 1907

gives is one of dignified solidity. It is curved on the corner and rusticated on the base. The observer looking for interesting architectural features is not disappointed. In the centre of the facade to Robinson Road a triple bay has giant free standing columns with balconies behind. These curved balconies between the columns have pretty, black wrought iron railings on them.

The Adelphi Hotel (1904), Stamford House (1900) and the John Little Building (1907) in Raffles Place were also built by Swan and MacLaren. With the exception of Stamford House none of these were the lasting landmarks that the more illustrious structures have become. The design of all three showed characteristic Bidwell grace with wide balconies on the Hotel, some regular pleasing plaster detailing in Stamford House (which mainly housed offices, with shops on the ground floor

opening on to the five foot way). The facade on John Little's Store was given a Dutch gable fronting the pitched roof. On the ground floor, the arches were flattened in the centre and the result is rather fussy. In those days the commercial and retail sections of town were not as divided from one another as they are today, so banks lived next door to the large shopping emporia. Raffles Place was shared by the Chartered Bank, the Mercantile Bank and by Robinson's and John Little's.

Between 1907 and 1912 Swan and MacLaren received a commission to rebuild St. Joseph's church, Victoria Street, in the Gothic style. The design work was prepared by another talented architect with the firm, David McLeod Craik, who joined them in 1907 and left in 1914 to fight in the First World War. The brief involved applying a Gothic skin to classical bones and the result was bound to be somewhat uneasy. The elevation of the building shows a classical disposition

John Little Building, Raffles Place. Swan and MacLaren, 1907, (top)

Stamford House, Stamford Road. Swan and MacLaren, 1900, (right)

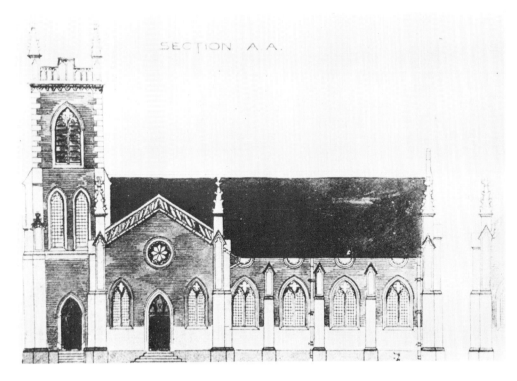

SECTION A.A.

Elevation, Wesley Methodist Church, Fort Canning Road, D. McLeod Craik, Swan and MacLaren, 1909, (top)

St. Joseph's Church, Victoria Street. D. McLeod Craik, Swan and MacLaren, 1907–12, (bottom)

Eu Villa, Mount Sophia. 1913

of architectural features in a regular manner. All the openings in the exterior were given pointed Gothic arches. The main and side towers, octagonal in shape, were faced with blind arcading out of which rose intricate cupolas. Inside this simple church hall the architectural features were kept to a minimum, decorative interest being vested in the statuary and panels of the Stations of the Cross. The original teak pews installed at this time are still in place, as is a splendid Gothic pulpit from Ceylon. However, the main and side altars of marble with low reliefs evoke a classical rather than a Gothic feeling.

Craik also had an opportunity to build a Gothic church from scratch for the Methodists on a beautiful site in the centre of town, the Wesley Methodist Church. Completed in 1909, it stands above the museum on Fort Canning Hill.

The Wesleyans were active missionaries and their first church had been built in 1858. The one at Fort Canning Rise is the second. It has been aptly described as toned down Gothic Revival. The church was built of red brick with some pretty Gothic tracery and mullion details in white stone or stucco. Inside it has some impressive wooden cross beams. In the 1960's the length of the church was doubled when an extension was built. Now the facilities have been further improved by the construction of a multipurpose hall beside the church in a utilitarian modern style which uses the same combination of brick and plaster work as the main church. This helps the new and old buildings to blend together.

Perhaps in the early years of the 20th Century more eclecticism in architectural design was fashionable in Singapore. There is much evidence to support this view, not least in the very grand Eu Villa built in 1913. It cost its owner $1,000,000. Song Ong Siang mentions that "it was

Government Printing Office (Attorney General's Chambers), High Street. c. 1910

built on an ideal spot and occupied a conspicuous position. The handsome furniture was supplied by well-known firms in Paris and London, while the marble statues are fine examples of Florentine art." The house was very much the Victorian villa with elements from many eras of architecture. Some Elizabethan details can be seen in the bay window to the front of the main entrance which is surmounted by a gable. This stood in front- of an imposing tower capped by a cupola. To the other side of the entrance was a two storey rotunda covered by a rather pointed roof, owing a debt to Edwin Lutyens. A classical segmental pediment of white stone marks the front entrance. To one side a sitting room on columns is a quotation from the Malay house in the manner of the Istana. The whole is very grand, its eclecticism in keeping with the essence and feeling of Singapore architecture.

1913 also saw Swan and MacLaren design the very attractive Jinrickshaw Station in Neil Road whose dominant feature is a curved corner elevation raised an extra storey above the roof, with a lantern on top. Then the First World War intervened, bringing a certain amount of economic hardship and a recession in building.

Although Swan and MacLaren seem to have dominated the architectural scene early in this century, many other worthy buildings were also being constructed. In Hill Street, the Central Fire Station was built in 1909. This splendidly cheerful red brick building with white rusticated banding has remained a treat for the eye as one rounds the corner from River Valley Road. The plans mark the architect as William Ferguson. The original part of the building, now at the left side, was built with horse drawn fire carts in mind. The central tower was used for drying hoses. A side extension in the same style was added in 1926. At this time the fire service was mechanized and garaging facilities were provided for motorized fire

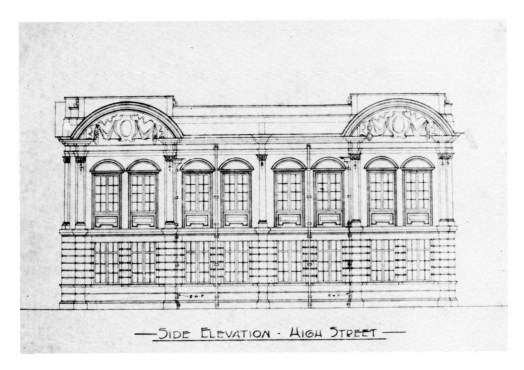

—SIDE ELEVATION · HIGH STREET—

Side elevation, Government Printing Office,   *Central Fire Station, Hill Street.*
High Street. c. 1910, (top)   *W. Ferguson, 1909, (bottom)*

Hotel de l'Europe, St. Andrew's Road, 1905.

engines. Later in the 1950's a further extension towards Fort Canning Road was constructed in the style of the municipal buildings of the time, again using red bricks, with a narrow horizontal overhang just below the roof line creating the impression of an attic storey. This wing is not just a rectangular box, but is stepped back from the facade in three steps, giving it personality but blending it with the main part of the building.

Opposite the Hotel de l'Europe and next to the Parliament House in High Street the Public Works Department built a Government Printing Office. In records held by the PWD the evolution of the planning process of this building is clearly shown. In the first instance the main entrance was to have opened on to High Street, with a portico above, standing from the building. The attic storey and balustrade hid three pitched roofs with valley gutters and only one curved seg-

mental pediment was designed for one end of the facade. Then the architect changed his mind, moved the entrance round the corner of the building and designed two segmental pediments for the High Street facade instead of one. There are also plans for a later extension to the building in the same style. The PWD used this building after the Government Printing Office was moved and remained there until 1976 when its offices in Maxwell Road were ready. At that point the building became the Attorney-General's Chambers and remains so today. The new accommodation for these two services gives further indication that Singapore was steadily becoming more civic-minded.

The great growth in wealth in these early years of the century meant that hospitals too were being developed and expanded. After being sited in such insalubrious locations as the swampy Balestier Plain, the Tan Tock Seng Hospital finally found its permanent home in Moulmein Road, off Thomson

Chartered Bank, Raffles Place. 1915, (top)

Convent of the Holy Infant Jesus, Victoria Street. Father Nain, 1910, (bottom)

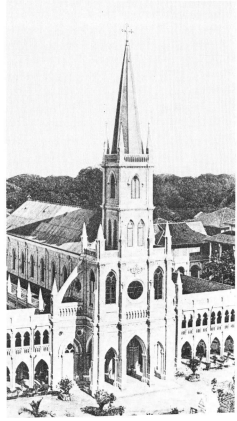

Road in 1909. This hospital today is basically a cluster of British colonial houses around a 1950's administration block, and the independence of the departments in different houses and buildings has been retained.

Having the atmosphere of a large cottage hospital, it is now a centre for lung diseases and neurology.

With the major increase in population at this time, markets needed to be larger and more permanent than before. The largest markets in Singapore, the Tekka Market in Buffalo Road and the Serangoon Market, were built in 1915 just after the start of the First World War.

Education also clearly prospered for although the Convent of the Holy Infant Jesus had been active since 1854, the school had been without a fitting house to worship in until this time. In 1910 a new church was built for the use of the Sisters and the pupils. A Catholic priest, Father Nain, who had worked on St. Joseph's Institution and knew his European architectural styles well, designed the chapel in the Gothic style. He even made an effort at buttressing, certainly for show rather than necessity.

A splendid Gothic arcade was erected, uniting all the elements of the Convent. Passageways from the chapel to the classrooms and from the chapel to the nun's house were all Gothicized. Even the back facade of Mr Caldwell's house was arcaded with pointed arches to fit in with the style of the chapel. Underneath the pointed arches, the porch of the house feels as classical as ever it did. Inside the chapel fine leaded stained glass windows of the apostles can be seen in the two aisles. The nave has a high apse and the plan is a conventional tripartite composition. A wooden balcony was built at the west end over the entrance. Some Malay woodwork is found in roundels and corbels in the ceilings of the aisles. The fine teak pews are original and have now been

taken to the new convent in Toa Payoh. All the statuary has gone too and the nuns were apparently as unsentimental about leaving the old convent as many Singaporeans seem to be about their old buildings. The convent contains two schools, run in English and Chinese. Buildings were added in 1906 to provide more classrooms and the last addition was a building on Stamford Road which was originally a home for refugees. The future of the convent hangs in the balance. The chapel has been gazetted a national monument, but the fate of Mr Caldwell's splendid house is uncertain. Part of the site will bow to the construction of the MRT and the station at Raffles City. The fabric of the church is not very stable and it is hoped that it will survive the vibration that construction entails.

With booming business in the early years of this century demand for new and more luxurious hotels also grew. In the same street but on the opposite side, on the site where the Supreme Court now stands, Singapore's largest hotel was built in 1905. The Hotel de l'Europe was four generous storeys high and its great size presented an impression of dignity and opulence. A heavy base supported the upper storeys and inside the accommodation stretched to 120 rooms, a large hall on the ground floor and a luxury roof garden. Its prominent location meant that it was the choice for many celebrations in the centre of the city.

By 1915, in a prominent position at one end of Raffles Place, the Chartered Bank's second building was completed. This was more pompous and perhaps more inspiring of security but less elegant than the former headquarters. The dome over the main entrance on the corner of the building was grand but overpowering giving the building an unbalanced air. The facade consisted of freestanding giant order columns between recessed windows. Terminating each end the pilastered bays

Gopuram, Sri Mariamman Temple today

Interior, Our Lady of Lourdes, Ophir Road, 1888, (opposite)

Interior, Church of St. Gregory the Illuminator, Hill Street. G.D. Coleman, 1835

Windows, Terraced House, Little India.
c. 1910, (top)

Terraced House, Blair Road. c. 1925,
(opposite)

Terraced houses, Emerald Hill Road. 1901,
(bottom)

Roof detail, Hong San See Temple,
Jalan Mohammed Sultan,
1913, (top)

Gothic Colonnade, Convent of the Holy
Infant Jesus, Victoria Street, Father Nain,
1910, (bottom)

Detached house, Alexandra Park. c. 1930
(top)

Nurses Home, Singapore General Hospital,
Outram Road, 1953, (bottom)

OCBC Centre, Chulia Street. I.M. Pei, 1976

did not have strong enough elements to counteract the weight of the dome. The weight of the rusticated basement was increased by balconies under the major bays. One regrets the passing of the older building. The inhabitants of Singapore have been historically unsentimental about the impermanence of buildings, and older structures have always been ruthlessly demolished when their usefulness has been outgrown. The second Chartered Bank building was demolished in 1952 and today a skyscraper stands in its place. The Bank's attitude is perhaps just a reflection of the pragmatic view of a practical commercial people that, where space is limited, one cannot afford to limp along with buildings that are outmoded.

The growing trade base of Singapore and Malaya developed at a time when Imperial rivalries were continuing round the globe. In defence of security the British army was now building extensive barracks in various parts of Singapore. The Tanglin Barracks, first started in the last years of the 19th Century, were a major affair, with large houses for officers and gracious messes for their recreation built on the hills around the former plantations. In Ridley Park off Tanglin Road many of the houses, which were built over a number of years, still stand today. These were designed for the tropical environment with pitched hipped or half hipped roofs, high ceilings, large rooms, tiled floors, cooled naturally by the tropical breezes with slowly revolving ceiling fans to help nature along. Sanitation was installed in the early years of this century and the Ridley Park houses were some of the first to benefit from the modern conveniences.

The army also needed a new church and in 1913 St. George's Church, Tanglin was built. Its exterior is austere red brick with minimal white stone decoration and a simple cross to identify its religious purpose. From the outside it represents the security of the church rather than its poetry. Two verandahs open on the nave of the church and are half open themselves to the garden surrounding the church; an ingenious adaptation of the nave and aisle plan of the conventional Christian church to the tropical climate. All the ornamentation on the interior is of relief brickwork, save for some wooden openwork panels made to imitate wrought iron. Captain Stanbury of the Royal Engineers began the work of the building of the church in 1910 and the total cost was Pounds 2,000. Its splendid stained glass windows bear the arms of British regiments serving in Singapore, flanking a suitably martial looking Christ. Captain Stanbury may have felt some of the influence of Edwin Lutyens, the master builder. In brick, in his houses, Lutyens achieved the superb sculptural decorative effects that are achieved in a more minor way in St. George's church. During the Second World War, the original church was used as an ammunition dump and the original stained glass windows were buried somewhere in the grounds, never to be recovered afterwards.

The population of the Chinese community continued to grow, a large number of immigrants arriving every year. Statistics for the years 1907, 1909 and 1911 give some indication of the volume: 227,000, 152,000 and 270,000 respectively. 1911 was a year of famine in China. The immigrants packed into overcrowded houses in Chinatown and the central areas of town where disease was rife, and sanitation facilities rudimentary. Today the remaining houses in this area bear the scars of their heavy use and physical neglect.

The more fortunate immigrant, with either good contacts or financial backing, could make an excellent life for himself in Singapore and join those Chinese and Straits Chinese who had already achieved prosperity.

The Chinese were indeed expanding their fortunes during this period. Although the English controlled the major banks and the financing, most of the business concerns were in the hands of Chinese families. Many of the wealthiest businessmen were Straits Chinese, locally born, who prospered under the British and were given great community responsibility by them. Eu Tong Sen, Tan Yeok Nee and Tan Jiak Kim were examples of such men. Their houses, however, were more often built in the European style and the Chinese house was the exception.

Middle class Chinese who were well off, and whose predecessors had made their homes in the Telok Ayer Street area, now started to move to new parts of town in this period. New areas such as Blair Road, Spottiswoode Park Road, Neil Road, Emerald Hill, Saunders Road, and Hullet Road were laid out by 1920 and there was a great growth in private housing. Speculative housing ventures were undertaken in streets in the Serangoon Road area as well as in Desker Road, in Syed Alwi Road off Jalan Besar, and in Geylang. In the two latter areas the developers were just as likely to have been Malay as Chinese or Straits Chinese. One particular Geylang entrepreneur excelled himself in decorating his houses in Lorong 19 with stucco reliefs of soldiers and guards. Even further away in Katong row houses were also built, fine examples existing in Koon Seng Road and Tembeling Road and some particularly fine shophouses were built in Joo Chiat Road.

From the beginning of the century until the 1920's the delightful vogue for extravagant decoration on the traditional terrace house was at its peak. The first roads in the Emerald Hill area were laid down in 1901, and from then on for three decades many plots were bought and developed as speculative enterprises by the Straits Chinese or built on and lived in by their owners. Many of the architects of the Emerald Hill houses are known, one

St. George's Church, Minden Road. Capt.
Stanbury, Royal Engineers, 1910–13,
(opposite)

Terraced houses, Emerald Hill Road.
c. 1925, (above)

Corner House, Joo Chiat Road and Koon
Seng Road. 1928, (bottom right)

Detail of stucco work, Lorong 19, Geylang. c. 1929

very fine tiles, imported from France and Belgium, and applied in great profusion to the walls and the pillars of the terraced houses. Roses, flowers and birds abound, often as an accompaniment to splendid relief stucco decoration on the facades in Chinese motifs of crabs and deer, dragons and mythical dogs, all splendid symbols of happiness, good fortune and long life.

The rich Chinese were not the only ones accumulating sufficient wealth at this time to be remembered in old photos and street names. The somewhat less wealthy and the other races were doing well with their speculative building, particularly for commercial purposes. For instance, a Muslim speculator erected a terrace of butcher houses in Syed Alwi off Jalan Besar which marks the culmination of the Singapore eclectic extravaganza. The plot sizes are more generous than the average and the ground floor ceilings are higher. Ventilation grates with Malay-inspired carved motifs stretch right across the width of the house, rather than being confined to the usual ventilation holes. On the upper floor, instead of the usual French window with the semicircular or curved fan light so prevalent in Singapore, we see oriole windows, oval in shape with a Baroque scroll at the bottom just to remind us of their European origin. The architect's clerk responsible must have been looking at a book on Baroque architecture when he decided to give his client something different. However he was not troubled about fitting in oval windows for he has ignored the problem and used conventional rectangular ones. In the full length French window in the centre of the facade, instead of Malay carved balustrades, one sees some of the lacy wrought iron balustrades which would have come out as ballast on the ships from England. Most of the iron-work made its way to Australia, to Sydney and Melbourne, but some stopped at Singapore.

of the best being W. B. Westerhout from Malacca. Splendid stucco decoration such as swags and floral designs were applied to the facades. Fine wood carving graced the upstairs balustrades, the fence doors (called *pintu pagar*) and the main doors, and sometimes also the airvents above the windows on the ground floor facade. The fascia boarding of the roof provided a fertile opportunity for decorative carving in the Malay style that the Straits Chinese loved. Fancy decoration touched everything that the Straits Chinese possessed, from the floral motifs on their sarongs, to the beaded embroidered slippers the women wore on their feet. Intricate carving in Malay, European and Chinese motifs found its way onto their furniture as well, and fine examples can still be seen today.

Outside these homes one often finds

Windows, Syed Alwi Road. c. 1920, (top)   *Palladian Window, Victoria Street, c. 1920, (bottom)*

In many areas we see that the speculators liked to make a feature of the corner of a house by cutting it off diagonally and putting on a balcony or special fenestration. Individual architectural features abound. For instance one finds the Venetian motif in every variation as a way of splitting up the three part front wall, although some are rather more faithful to Venetian architecture than others. Other facades are more simply Georgian but these are just as attractive as the very florid or abundantly decorated stucco facades with tile inlay work. Most of these houses built as speculative ventures were in terraces, so the facades have continuity. Alas, this delightful and uniquely Singaporean decorative style· was soon to slip into decline. Many of the Straits Chinese sons were educated in England and they brought back European ways in attitudes and dress. As the pace of life became faster the intricate crafts that the women practised and the fashions for embroidery, beaten silver and woodcarving slowly died out. By the end of the First World War Chinese weddings were taking place in western white dress and after the 1920's the Chinese houses sadly became more austere, following the pattern of the times.

Steadily increasing wealth enabled the Chinese to build more temples of note at this time. One such temple was the Hong San See, relocated to Jalan Mohammed Sultan off River Valley Road in 1913. The large warehouses belonging to United Engineers had not yet grown up. The temple is indeed on a steep site as the long flights of steps prove. When the temple is reached it is a feast for the eyes. The visitor is greeted with beautiful carving on the brackets and posts supporting the roof. Inside some more exquisite carving meets the eye under the purlins, the eaves of the roof and along the roof ridge. The comparatively large courtyards and main and side pavilions give a greater sense of the traditional Chinese enclosure than other temples such as Tan Si Chong Su in Magazine Road.

All the hard work of fortune building left a need for recreational facilities. Katong was the haven for weekenders from the civil services, Europeans and Straits Chinese, indeed for anyone who had the money and the inclination to escape on weekends to peace and quiet from crowded workaday Singapore. Seaside bungalows were built in Tanjong Rhu for civil servants. Houses grew up along such roads as Marine Parade and East Coast Road. Some houses may still be seen today among the fast burgeoning blocks of high rise flats along the East Coast. The Straits Chinese also built weekend bungalows in the area stretching from Tanjong Rhu to Joo Chiat Road. The gardens extended to the water's edge where there were private jetties for access to the sea. The modern reclamation projects of the 1970's and 80's were still 50 years away.

Many of the bungalows were elegant, some larger, others wider, longer and lower than their counterparts in River Valley Road or Tanglin. Wide verandahs had a view of the sea and steps led to the garden. Some of these houses stood on stilts for improved coolness. Little difference can be noted between the Straits Chinese and the European bungalow except in the decoration and the detail. For instance, a Chinese house would never be painted in black and white, as to the Chinese these colours signify death and mourning.

It may be illuminating to give a word of background about the origin of these houses once so typical of colonial South East Asia. These old houses, whether colonial, Chinese, Indian or Malay had features in common which were derived from the considerations of providing shelter in a tropical environment. The buildings had to be cool, to be

*Hong San See Temple, Jalan Mohammed
Sultan, 1913, (top)*

*Bungalow, Tanjong Katong. c. 1910,
(bottom)*

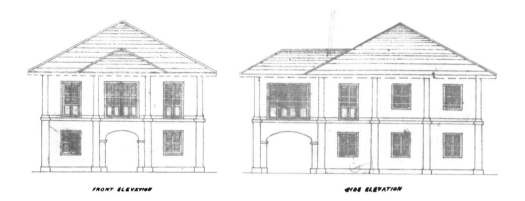

FRONT ELEVATION   SIDE ELEVATION

Elevation, House for Inche Abdul Rahmin at New Harbour Road. 1894, (top)

Belle Vue, Oxley Rise. c. 1840, (bottom)

waterproof, to withstand the severe battering of monsoon rain and to exclude the hot sun from the interior rooms. Lastly, they had to provide a degree of protection from the insect and reptile life that flourishes in these parts.

As mentioned previously, the Malays, as indigenous builders, mastered all these problems. They raised their houses off the ground and made them out of durable, white ant-proof woods. They covered them with high pitched, overhanging attap or wood roofs. This type of house design was eminently practical and the early European settlers in Singapore followed this pattern, until safety and social pressures demanded a more permanent and dignified architectural style.

With certain adaptations, Coleman's Palladian-inspired houses, along with the large and grand neo-classical plantation houses, were prototypes for the next suburban compound houses. Classical decorations were combined with a Malayan house plan to produce the most successful though rather plain blend of Anglo-Singaporean detached house, with bricks and later concrete square columns to support the house. Roofs were steep, with overhanging eaves, but in place of attap, Chinese red roof tiles or square grey tiles were used. Walls were often left open or half closed-in, with large openings that could be covered with louvred shutters or chick blinds when the weather turned inclement. The verandah so often seen on the Malay house was extended and given more prominence as a carriage porch, usually with a large room above it which housed the main living area. This room had cross ventilation and usually remained one of the coolest rooms in the house. Bedrooms were built on either side of the verandah and behind it, with dining facilities in the middle of the house. Wooden floors were retained on the upper floor with marble or tiles for the ground

floor, if there was one. The kitchen and servants' quarters were situated a short distance from the back of the house and linked to it by a covered walkway. Sometimes, an extra semi-circular room with bay windows was attached to one end of the house. This, like the front porch, is another Malay inspired appendage, called a *balai peranginan,* and it was originally intended as a room where guests could be received, or stay. It appears more on Straits Chinese houses, especially in the Katong area, but some European houses also have it.

This basic house design had two distinct types of decoration. Simplified classical elements of decoration such as columns, pilasters and rustication followed in the footsteps of the large plantation houses. Sir Thomas Oxley's Belle Vue and the Kampung Glam Istana, both dating from the early 1840's, are good examples of this prototype. So too is the present day Istana, although on a very much grander scale, built in 1869 by Captain J. F. A. McNair, the First Colonial Engineer, to replace the old Raffles Government House on Fort Canning. With a blend of classic details and tropical layout based on the Malay house, it is a prime example of the type of Anglo-Singaporean house that remained popular right through to the 1930's. Often built for members of the Civil Service or for employees of the established companies in Singapore, there are many examples still in existence. Civil service estates such as Pender Road, Seton Close and Malcolm Road; army estates such as Ridley Park and Goodwood Hill; or private company compounds such as Cable Road for MacAlisters Trading Company, Firestone Park for Firestone Rubber Company or Institution Hill for United Engineers, all have houses painted in black and white. The inspiration for these black and white houses is to be found in the sprawling suburbs of England where Stockbroker-belt

Government House (Istana). Capt. J.F.A. McNair, 1869, (top)

Adis Lodge, House of F.D. Almeida. c. 1880, (bottom)

Mount Echo, Sri Menanti Estate. c. 1920,
(top)

Detached House, Cairnhill Road. c. 1910,
(bottom)

Detached House, Goodwood Hill. c. 1920

Tudor housing, under the inital influence of the Arts and Crafts movement of the late 19th Century, became the dominant feature of the early 20th Century suburban housing.

In India too, this Tudor spirit was copied endlessly for the Hill Station bungalows. In Poona, Ootacamund, and Simla, the same houses can be seen. The wooden divisions of the walls, however, also betray influences closer to home. Many Indonesian, Malay and Burmese indigenous houses have the same divisions which support and strengthen the matting walls. It is a small jump of the imagination from that to the Tudor-style timbered divisions.

Another distinct group of houses show markedly less British influence. The Dutch houses of Singapore are direct copies of those in Indonesia and Malacca and are characterized by outward sloping (battered) brick and stuccoed walls, heavily-eaved swooping tiled roofs and large semicircular windows on the ground floor which are nearly always decorated with fancy radiating brickwork. The houses, which are on two storeys, are seldom found in large compounds as are the other types of houses. The Chartered Bank owned some houses in this style in Dalvey Road and Cluny Road. They also own houses in this style in Belmont Road and Cornwall Gardens, actually built by a German architect working in this style in the 1930's.

Anglo-Singaporean house building continued into the 1930's with the same basic shape and layout but in this decade they were seldom painted black and white. Houses for senior civil servants in Mount Pleasant Road and the houses in Alexandra Park built for the army in 1936 and 1937 fit into this category. More modern houses nestled in between the older larger houses in the Sri Menanti

Belmont House, Belmont Road. c. 1930,
(top)

No. 1, Dalvey Estate,.
(bottom)

121

Estate for the Hongkong Shanghai Bank in Jervois Road. All that exists today of the estate is Mount Echo, mouldering but grandly opulent, and much missing its former occupant, the head of the Bank.

Finally, the growth of trade was putting pressure on commercial facilities once again. By the end of the 19th Century all the space available for godowns on the river was used up. In about 1905 the alternatives to the ox cart started to appear and the godowns no longer found it essential to be by the water, although most of them remained in the river area. A group of splendid brick warehouses with Dutch Gables was built near Read Bridge between the river and River Valley Road, and one godown with Chinese roofs nearby must at one time have been a private house.

The first two decades of the 20th Century in Singapore saw many changes, yet the continuity of life and architecture from the 19th Century was still tangible. In the next twenty years many changes were to be seen in building methods and architectural aesthetics accompanying the social changes of the inter-war period.

Dutch godown, off River Valley Road.
c. 1920

PERIOD OF TRANSITION
1920 — 1940

After the First World War an immediate short-lived boom gave way to a brief slump in 1920. By 1923, however, this translated itself into the greatest boom that Singapore had ever enjoyed. The tin and rubber prices in Malaya reached new heights in 1926 and 1927 and several businessmen — such as Tiger Balm King Aw Boon Haw and rubber magnate Lee Kong Chian — made huge fortunes in a very short time. By the end of the decade the Great Depression hit Singapore, with a crumbling of commodity prices and capital values.

On the surface Singapore was little affected either by World War One or by the Chinese revolution, but ultimately these two events changed her history. The inter-war years were deceptively calm, marked by a steady separation of the colonial officials and European expatriates from the Asians in the community, and an increased snobbishness, complacency and blindness to what was going on around them. In most ways this was really the twilight of the Empire, ultimately shattered by World War II.

In the 1920's unprecedented prosperity saw a considerable rise in government spending, with several large building projects for the administration, for the police, education and medical services. Increased health care, better water facilities and sewage systems all helped to decrease the incidence of the most basic diseases born of filth, overcrowding and hot climate. The municipal ordinance ensured that more money was kept for improvements in roads, electricity supply and municipal cleanliness.

Perhaps the most profound changes, however, occurred through the increase in people's mobility. The period saw a growth in public transport, the arrival for the well-to-do of the family car and the early development of regular air travel. The resulting adjustments to Singapore were as great as for any city at the time.

The Johore causeway was opened in 1923, carrying road and rail traffic. The Singapore Traction Company was set up in 1925 to operate trolleys and omnibuses. The number of motor cars had increased from 842 in 1915 to 3,605 in 1920 and for several years there was chaos on the roads, which the Municipality resurfaced to cope with the heavier traffic. While the centre of town was already very congested, more and more office buildings rose out of the ground and increasing numbers of immigrants crowded into Chinatown.

In most ways, however, these were times of rapid improvement in the quality of life for the better off. In the early 1920's electricity had been a rarity outside the centre of town. In 1927, the first power station opened at St James's, spreading electric light to a wider area. Food supplies increased. The Singapore Cold Storage Company manufactured its first ice-cream in 1920 and in 1926 it

*Interior, Railway Station, Keppel Road.
1932, (top)*

*Railway Station, Keppel Road. 1932,
(bottom)*

Municipal Building (City Hall), St. Andrew's Road. F.D. Meadows, 1926-29

became the sole manufacturer of ice. In the same year it set up a pig farm and in 1929 a dairy farm at Bukit Timah. The next year it began to produce bread and in 1933 set up a groceries department, importing vegetables from the Cameron Highlands, meat from New Zealand, fruit from South Africa and the United States, and groceries from Europe. The same general mix of consumables is, incidentally, available at Cold Storage today. The population could also enjoy beer as never before as Malayan Breweries established a brewery in Alexandra Road in 1932.

Architecturally, this period divides itself naturally into two sections: the 1920's with the last flowering of classical and colonial architecture; and the 1930's with the first of the Modern Movement buildings. In the 1930's Singapore suffered quite severely from the Depression and rather less was built in this decade than in the boom years of the 20's.

In many ways the most impressive buildings of the 1920's were the major municipal and public developments. We have already noted the opening of the Johore Causeway, connecting Singapore by road and railway with the Malay Peninsula. The railway brought further prosperity to Singapore and clearly needed to be marked by a suitably impressive railway terminus. This was built at Keppel Road in 1932. Sir Cecil Clementi Smith opened it with a speech referring to it as "a Terminus of world importance". The construction took three years and it has been claimed that the architect was influenced by Eliel Saarinen's Helsinki Station. It was built of reinforced concrete in a stripped, utilitarian classical style but with a distinct grace in the wide arches, the lofty inner spaces and the 72 foot dome. Exposed arches in the central booking hall emphasise its purity of line. Between the arches are interesting panels of ceramic tiles fired by Doulton and Co. and depicting local scenes such as shipping, tin mining, copra planting, paddy planting, and other Malayan activities. On the exterior facade of the station four heroic figures represent Commerce, Agriculture, Industry and Shipping.

Towards the end of the 1920's the Municipal Building itself was erected on the Padang. It occupied the site of two houses which had belonged to Thomas Church and Dr Montgomery in the early

General Post Office (Fullerton Building), Fullerton Road. Keyes and Dowdeswell, 1928

days of Singapore, and which had later been requisitioned for municipal offices. This was by far the largest public building to be built to-date. The architect was F. D. Meadows, who created an unpretentious but dignified building with simple lines and uncomplicated massing. When the Hotel de l'Europe was still standing they looked rather like cousins, the younger cousin rather more pompous, more serious than the older one. A substantial basement supports the building with wide rusticated bands, and a very wide staircase in the centre emphasizes the height of the podium. On the first and second levels the regular rows of windows are set behind a free standing colonnade all along the front of the building, creating a satisfactory sense of depth and shade. At either end the facade is terminated by a heavier wall and window arrangement standing forward. This gives a satisfying air of finality to the building. Above the architrave a balustrade stands above the roof. The steps of the municipal building have been the scene of several momentous occasions in Singapore's history. On this spot Lord Louis Mountbatten accepted the surrender of

the Japanese after World War II, and Prime Minister Lee Kuan Yew declared the independence of Singapore in 1959.

Another new and imposing building, to house the General Post Office, was built on the site of the former Fort Fullerton. This is the Fullerton Building, designed by Keyes and Dowdeswell and completed in 1928. The General Post Office itself used the two ground floors for sorting rooms, postal halls and offices; and the upper floors were occupied by the Singapore Club for their facilities. Two interior courts gave light to the Postal Hall and light and ventilation to the interior courts upstairs. The Club required dining rooms, club rooms, billiards and card rooms, and had sleeping accommodation on the upper floors. These bedrooms explain the attic story above the parapet and the rather incongruous domestic aspect this presents in what is essentially a public building. Now the Fullerton Building is occupied by the GPO and government offices, and the Singapore Club survives no longer.

At this time the police force modernized itself, learning to deal effectively with the almost constant fighting between rival street gangs in Chinatown. Several Police buildings were constructed, among them the Hill Street Police Station

Hill Street Police Station, Hill Street. F. Dorrington Ward, 1927

CID Building, Cecil Street. F. Dorrington Ward, 1929, (top)

Customs House, Maxwell Road. F. Dorrington Ward, 1930, (bottom)

129

in 1927. F. Dorrington Ward, PWD architect constructed this building under Government Hill opposite the site of Whampoa's Ice House. This was the first tall building in Singapore and accommodated housing for policemen as well as the police station itself. Its wrap-around-the-corner design is inspired, as are the three angled sections of the building. The total rustication of the facade — now reduced to a pure decorative element — adds distinction, and the overhanging closed balconies and roofline suggest the tropical architecture and the modesty balconies of a Muslim society. The massive scrolls which support them bring us firmly back to the Renaissance. As with the Supreme Court of ten years later, Dorrington Ward has played with the High Renaissance form, the soberness of colour contrasting with playful use of details. The relatively unadorned triangular interior courtyard is not so impressive. This building is now undergoing a change in use as the Police have left and government agencies such as the Archives and Oral History Department have moved in.

Two years later Dorrington Ward built another Police building, the Detective Headquarters on the corner of Cecil Street and Robinson Road. A more conventional building, on a courtyard plan, it still stands today.

In this last flowering of colonialism more government departments sprang up, all requiring officials and civil servants. To this end, as municipal architect Dorrington Ward built the Customs House and Post Office on Maxwell Road in 1930. In its simplicity this building has much more of a familiar 1920's atmosphere to it than, say, the Supreme Court or the Hill Street Police Station. A round tower marks the corner entrance to the building with a very shallow dome covering it. Contemporary drawings held by the HDB show that the windows were originally wooden, surmounting vertical

panels. When the building was later air-conditioned, metal windows were installed and the decoration of the panels changed to the distinctive sunbursts one sees today.

At the turn of the decade the Ministry of Labour building was completed. Singapore's labour relations were not run on the same lines as in England, but rudimentary labour societies began to exist around this time. The Ministry, built for the Chinese Protectorate, was designed in a stripped classical style, with a characteristic string course projecting below the roofline, an attic above it, and art deco inspired decorations on the columns where the capitals once would have been. In plan and shape this building is well conceived, with an interesting play of planes and angles.

The Edward VII School of Medicine, on the site of the Outram General Hospital, now the Singapore General Hospital, was designed by Keys and Dowdeswell. It has been described as "a typical design from this partnership which specialized in massive florid works in the new classic tradition". A substantial colonnade greets the visitor, behind which stand a series of bronze doors leading into the centre of the building and the library. Above the entablature of the colonnade is a rather peculiar attic storey with dormer windows. These are curiously domestic in character, perching above such a grand facade. Altogether, though, this is a less complicated and more satisfactory design than the Fullerton Building. Although the exterior looks classical, the building was actually built of reinforced concrete.

In 1926, the old iron bridge which had been built in 1863 and named after Lord

Ministry of Labour, Havelock Road. 1930, (top)

Edward VII School of Medicine, Singapore General Hospital, Outram Road. Keys and Dowdeswell, 1927, (bottom)

Elgin, the then reigning Governor General of India, had outlived its usefulness. A double concrete bridge with a graceful curving iron superstructure was built to replace it. It connected the Chinese community on the south side of the river with the Indian merchants of High Street on the north side. At the two ends of the bridge are some elegant iron lampstands and roundels with the Singapura lion cast into them. They were produced by Cavaliere Nolli who was to carve the capitals and tympanum of the Supreme Court a decade later.

This period was clearly one of transition for architecture in Singapore. One sees a mixture of styles appearing, usually in relation to the use of the building. Government buildings and banks exhibit the last vestiges of grand classicism, although even there the old conventions of decoration and proportion were breaking down. The new Hongkong and Shanghai Bank Building in Fullerton Square was an example of this. Completed in 1925 by Swan & MacLaren, it incorporated the site of the building next door, the Deutsche Asiatische Building. Its box-like character stood in sober contrast to the extravagant former building and the rectangularity of its form was barely masked by the simple classical details. The tower perched uncomfortably on its roof. This building and its more imaginative neighbour on Collyer Quay, the Ocean Building, built in 1930, had reinforced concrete frames and their style formed a transition between the Victorian classicism from which they sprang and the simplicity of buildings influenced by the Modern Movement.

The very last example of British Imperial architecture was built by the PWD on the Padang nearly a decade later, in 1937-9. The Supreme Court building was F. Dorrington Ward's last design in Singapore. For what he wished to build, he had only a small site to work on. He built his steel frame building as four blocks. These surrounded a central courtyard, housing the charming circular law library. He made the building as monumental as possible with all the conventions, but sadly in the end the site made the result rather cramped and unsatisfactory. The building and the dome are too high for the width of the building, and the classical facade decoration seems pasted on, without fitting into the fabric of the building. In the interior, the main stairway has neither enough width nor enough space for adequate emphasis, and one has the impression of going through a cave to get upstairs. However unsatisfactory the spatial arrangements may be, the details, arches and Georgian windows are very well proportioned. Revolutionary modern rubber tiles were laid in geometric motifs on the first floor to absorb the noise. The first floor housed the four original courts. A fifth has now been added on this floor, and three more on upper floors. However, the original courtrooms are more substantial in their decoration and more traditional. Wood panelling covers the walls and the traditional alcove marks the judge's chair. Behind the dock in these courts one can still see the trap door where the accused is led up from the cells down below. The most pleasing feature of the courthouse is the little library with its restrained white dome, its travertine columns holding up balconies on two levels, both lined with bookshelves. Lantern lights in the dome have been covered up but light enters from a row of windows at its base.

Above the entrance an Italian sculptor

Hongkong and Shanghai Bank, Fullerton Square. Swan and MacLaren, 1925, (top)

Supreme Court, St. Andrew's Road. F. Dorrington Ward, 1937–39, (bottom)

The Arcade (Rubber share brokers' den), Singapore.

Arcade, Collyer Quay. D. McLeod Craik, Swan and MacLaren, 1910 (top) and 1920 (bottom)

Cavaliere Nolli carved the pediment sculpture, an allegory of Justice. In reliefs around the entrance porch, a sculptor from the firm of Wagstaff and Sons executed local scenes of history and commerce of the Straits Settlements. In a newspaper article the architect stated that "the Supreme Court was built to harmonize with the City Hall next door, and the layout visualizes another Government building which will match the Municipal offices. The whole will eventually make an entity without equal in the East."

The government was also clearly feeling the need for some economy: "The building, although of an aspect both internally and externally calculated to strike awe in the minds of the populace could only be treated in an economic and reasonable manner, no attempt being made, for instance, to provide the usual marble panelling, flooring and decoration." The last classical building in Singapore, it was built by United Engineers Ltd.

The minority groups also contributed to the architecture of this period. Singapore has never been noted for a large quantity of Muslim buildings, but in the 1920's the conventional Arcade building, originally designed by Donald Craik of Swan and MacLaren, was given a new Islamic skin which earned it the reputation as one of the most remarkable office buildings in South East Asia. Its Dutch gables were translated into onion domes and moorish arches replaced the classical ones.

Several wealthy Arab families, such as the Alkaffs, the Alsagoffs and the Aljunieds had made fortunes trading in spices from the region and owning land in such areas as Geylang and Serangoon Road. Families such as these were also community-minded. In 1924, it was decided that the area around Arab Street needed a new mosque on the site of the original one, built in 1824. Swan and MacLaren were commissioned to design it and the Sultan Mosque opened its doors for worship in 1928. By far the largest mosque in Singapore, it has two large domes of the traditional Muslim shape, and many smaller ones. Arabic crenelations mark the roofline and many varied details contribute to an interesting roof silhouette. The proportions are, however, essentially balanced in the manner of Western architecture and the details are well researched for their authenticity. Inside, the decoration is minimal, with ogee arches for the two arcades which divide the building into three. The two side portions have the traditional separate galleries for women.

In 1925 the Hindu community extensively renovated the Sri Mariamman Temple in South Bridge Road. The *gopuram* was completely altered in shape and decoration, from the restrained levels of the former to the proliferation of sculpture on the latter.

In 1927 an event occurred which was to affect the appearance of all subsequent buildings. The Architects Ordinance required all buildings to be designed by qualified architects. One of the basic charms of earlier terraces had been the inevitable hybrids caused by a combination of untrained draughtsmen not understanding the logic of architectural detail and whimsical speculative builders who usually employed the draughtsmen after hours. From 1927 the architectural profession prospered and young men went to England to train there. Shophouses and terraces continued to be built, but now in a plainer, more austere, indeed more boring style, without the features that Singaporeans had come to recognize as their own.

The 1920's also saw the flowering of the great desire by many of the local population to emulate the Europeans. The old traditions of the Straits Chinese were dying out, replaced by European

Sultan Mosque, Muscat Street, Swan and MacLaren, 1824, (top)

Interior, Sultan Mosque, Muscat Street, Swan and MacLaren, 1824, (bottom)

customs of dress and similarly architecture. Many of the men who made their fortune in this decade built themselves European-type houses. For instance, Aw Boon Haw, who with his brother built the huge Tiger Balm empire, had a house built for himself in Nassim Road in 1924, using an American architect. The patron had wished it to look like the White House, Washington D.C. Several doors away, however, a gem of a Malay-inspired house still stands, reputedly built for one of his wives. Perhaps the womenfolk were less adventurous than the men.

In the 1930's the rage for new up-to-date architecture was responsible for the appearance of distinctive modern houses, such as those that grew up on the estate in Kay Siang Road. These were the first houses built in the modern style for Singapore Improvement Trust officials. Their rooms — comparatively small and low-ceilinged for the 1930's — look forward to the houses of the future: they were designed to be air-conditioned.

The reference in these houses is to modern ships and liners, a new and exciting form of transport. Rounded corners and metal windows are intentionally borrowed from the nautical vernacular. A large boarding house off Grange Road has such features on a much larger scale, with several smaller houses in the same style around it. These are tucked back off River Valley Road, and off St Thomas Walk. This is perhaps the first instance of the Western ideology overtaking the tropical rationale in architecture. In the 1980's we see this movement as a disease, with houses being designed solely for airconditioning and ignoring the ingenious blends of ventilation skills and lightness of architectural touch which had characterized domestic design up until this time.

For the poorer population, conditions had not improved. In 1927, the Singapore Improvement Trust (SIT) was set up to stem the slide of Singapore housing into complete slums. Their first task was to drive back lanes between the streets and behind the houses in Chinatown, in an effort to provide ventilation in this over-built area. They also undertook new building projects. Various estates were designed in the emerging style of "workers housing" which was to become so prevalent from the 1930's onwards. The architects who designed them had been looking at the new architecture of the French, such as Le Corbusier, and of the Dutch, Germans and British. Built of reinforced concrete with flat roofs and windows which wrapped around the corner, these new buildings spelt the promise of the future. Inside the flats were small and basic, but they provided much better shelter than the shanty towns and slums in which the majority of the poor had to live in Singapore. Some of the buildings in the early estates of Tiong Bahru, Princess Elizabeth Estate, Kallang, and Queenstown can still be seen today. Their tell-tale external aspect of hollow concrete blocks easily identify them. All the flats were walk-ups and at this time were usually only four storeys tall.

Modern travel was coming to Singapore along with the Modern Movement in architecture. The first airplane in Singapore was flown by a Frenchman in 1911 at Farrer Park, the site of the former Race Course. Singapore was a stopping-off place in the first England to Australia air race in 1919 and it became a regular transit stop for many pioneer aviators. By 1923 the Government had constructed a seaplane base at Sembawang near the proposed naval base, and a Royal Air Force base at Seletar. Seletar aerodrome was completed in the late 1920's and at first served civil aircraft as well as the R.A.F. A regular airmail service from London began in 1931, when Imperial

Aw House, Nassim Road. 1924,
(top)

Detached House, Nassim Road. c. 1920,
(bottom)

Detached House, Grange Road. c. 1930,
(top)

Detatched House, Kay Siang Road. c. 1937,
(bottom)

139

Airways and Qantas began weekly flights with Singapore as a stopover. Finally in 1937 a civil airport with a grass runway was opened at Kallang with daily flights to Kuala Lumpur, Ipoh and Penang, enabling speedy postal and newspaper delivery services.

The residents of the numerous kampungs at Kallang had to be relocated and the airfield to be cleared for this new aerodrome. The terminal building was steel framed, with continuous glass windows and long rounded balconies cantilevered outwards. These features, and the flat roof and standardized construction methods made it a monument to the Modern Movement. However, purism was only skin deep as inside, the hall was gleaming example of Art Deco, not at all up-to-date, but very impressive nonetheless.

The army built versions of the Modern Movement in their Changi estates, containing the Air Force Base and the Hospital. A jail was also built at Changi in 1936. A utilitarian structure, it has a rather Indian entrance, and a series of small Lutyens domes.

During the 1930's, the British Military presence in Singapore was again considerably increased, as was the number of civil servants. Two large residential parks were built, Alexandra Park and Barracks, and Portsdown Camp and military housing. Alexandra Park had more luxurious houses; both are notable for very imaginative and attractive landscaping. (The Hampshire regiment, which created Portsdown Road Camp, were noted for finding good sites and landscaping them with talent).

Despite these dramatic changes — the car, the aeroplane and the Modern Movement — not all was going well.

In 1932, the Depression in the West hit Singapore through the prices fetched for rubber and tin. From record heights in 1927, prices plummeted, rubber crashing from 34 cents to 4.95 cents in June 1932 and tin to $60.00 a picul. Singapore's revenues dropped drastically at a time when public expenditure was at a height, a great many public buildings being constructed. By 1932, hardship inevitably ensued. The government slashed salaries, dismissed officials, cut public works and health services, and increased taxation. All communities in Singapore were in a very depressed state.

However, with the slow revival of world confidence, Singapore recovered from the slump. Helped by higher taxation rates and more effective output, a balanced budget was once again achieved in 1933. The output of tin and rubber became more regulated in an effort to ensure that it should not go out of control again in the future.

The slump led to many changes in Chinese business methods, and the development and improvement of their own banking operations was one of these. The opening of the Oversea-Chinese Banking Corporation in Chulia Street was an example. Now an amalgamation of three former banks, it was housed in China Building, opened in 1932. Designed by Keys and Dowdeswell, the building had the distinctive Chinese features of a prominent roof and characteristic roof brackets. Vertical pilasters flanked the central door with incised Chinese characters. However, that was the extent of the Chinese flavour of this edifice. In essence it was Western with the interior galleries surrounding a central banking hall and working area. The facade was made rather fussy to look superficially Chinese. The building was demolished to make way for the OCBC Centre in 1976.

Just before the end of the decade the

SIT flats, Tiong Bahru. c. 1930, (top)

HDB Flats, 1st Generation, Ganges Avenue. c. 1960, (bottom)

first high-rise building in Singapore was constructed. The Cathay Building in Dhoby Ghaut was finished in 1939. Built by Frank Brewer, it was designed as a hotel. A subsequent glut of hotel space led to its transformation into an office building, both by filling in all the balconies, and making bay windows. It is now the headquarters of the Cathay Organisation.

Throughout this period Singapore's architectural development had continued strongly. A comment made by an American visitor in 1929, aptly captures the rapidity of growth in the first decades of the 20th Century. He said after eight years absence, "It is marvellous how you have progressed. Why I hardly know the place." (Luscome 1930). A familiar phrase today — and perhaps always — in this everchanging city.

With the approach of the Second World War, the pace slowed down; and when the Japanese entered Singapore all building ground to a halt. The next decade opened a new type of architecture for the last days of Colonial rule.

Kallang Airport. 1937, (above)

China Building, Chulia Street. Keys and Dowdeswell, 1931-32, (top right)

Cathay Building, Mount Sophia. F. Brewer, 1939, (bottom right)

Prinsep Court S.I.T. Flats 1948–9

MODERNISM TAKES HOLD
1940 — 1970

Although Singapore survived the war with relatively little physical damage, the social situation in terms of unemployment, overcrowding and lack of housing was serious. Economically it took two years of chaos before the colony began to get back on its feet. By 1947 the demand in the West for tin and rubber was once more high enough to give the economy of Singapore renewed impetus.

In the immediate post-war years the city centre in Chinatown had several families living in one house, with minimal sanitation and water facilities. Under such desperately overcrowded conditions, disease was rife. On the periphery of Chinatown, indeed in any available space, temporary dwellings were constructed of whatever material was available — bits of old metal, discarded tar paper. These shacks were hardly weather proof.

Once the economy was in a more stable condition, the Singapore Improvement Trust (SIT) continued the start it had made before the war. In the years 1948-49, nine blocks of SIT flats were designed in Sago Street, Prinsep Street and Tiong Bahru, by A. G. Church and Lincoln Page respectively. Flats in Upper Pickering Street were built in 1950-52 by S.C. Woolmer. New towns further away from the centre such as Queenstown were also constructed around 1952. An effort was made to produce mixed housing of different heights. These flats were very simple compared to architecture in the private sector but efforts were made to raise the level of design above mere building. Consideration was given to through draughts by making the buildings one-room wide; for this reason, these early flats often looked very long and narrow. Roofs were now flat, true to the dictates of Modern Movement architecture. The construction of the frame was of reinforced concrete with brick panel infill and hollow block floors. The roof was constructed separately from the main structure to allow for expansion and contraction due to changes in temperature.

As there was no allowance in modern architecture for ornamentation, visual interest was created by featuring balconies and staircases. In the flats in Upper Pickering Street, balconies occur only every fourth floor, and the intervening horizontal bands exist purely for visual effect. The staircase is expressed by prominent curved returns and diagonal sides. The support column is also clearly visible, topped by a projecting overhang from the roof which covers the top flight of stairs. These flats have been built on the diagonal, in the form of parallelograms rather than rectangles. Considering the inherent monotony of this type of building, a considerable variety and attention to form has been shown.

The efforts of the SIT unfortunately did little to alleviate the housing shortage, which had now reached chronic proportions. The Trust did not have enough con-

S.I.T. Flats, Upper Pickering Street S.C. Woolmer, 1950–52, (top left)

Flats, Clemenceau Avenue. D.C. Rae, 1949–51, (top right)

Flats, Clemenceau Avenue. W.I. Watson, 1951–53, (bottom left)

Flats, Nassim Hill. K.A. Brundel, 1950–51, (bottom right)

stitutional power to appropriate funds for compulsory purchase of land for its developments or for relocation of the population. However the colonial authorities were proud of the progress they had made. Their aim was to produce 12,000 units a year, and it is only with hindsight that history has proved their effort too limited. The growth in population continued to exceed the supply of flats and despite efforts to limit immigrant entry into Singapore, the problem could only worsen. Only in 1960 when the Housing and Development Board (HDB) was formed, with constitutional power to buy up land and relocate the residents, did enough flats begin to be built to ameliorate the housing situation.

In the early post-war years flats were also being built for government officials and civil servants. In 1950-53, D. C. Rae and W. I. Watson, City Architect and Building Surveyor respectively, designed some interesting units in Clemenceau Avenue. They were constructed of concrete and faced with brick. The horizontal emphasis created by the rows of balconies is typical of design of that period.

Three blocks at Nassim Hill for senior Government Officers were designed by K. A. Brundle, Chief Architect of the PWD in 1950-1. These flats consist of a long 4-storey rectangular block emphasized horizontally by the fenestration. Two projecting bays break forward, in the middle and at one end of the building. The key talent in designing modern buildings is the ability to relate the position and proportion of the parts one to another. No longer can decorative detail mask the front of a building. In the Nassim Hill flats and in the Nurses Home that Brundle built at the Singapore General Hospital in 1953, we see that the Modern Movement

Macdonald House, Orchard Road. Palmer and Turner, 1948–49

has truly taken hold. The Home consists of three five storeyed wings enclosing a rectangular courtyard and a two storeyed wing, which contains the dining room, recreation room, lounge and kitchen. The interest in this building lies in the combination of disparate elements, balancing each other rather asymmetrically, as in a sculpture.

At least the architects of this period remembered they were in the tropics and within the confines of the new universal aesthetic made provisions for the character of the climate. Prominent window lintels, often extended round the building as sunshade projections, and a fashion for framing windows with a deep, over-size projecting frame prevailed. These created interesting effects of light and shade, as well as protecting the interior from the heat. These features can still be seen in many buildings of this period.

The Odeon Cinema in North Bridge Road was built in a similar style, designed by the firm of architects Palmer and Turner who had emerged from Shanghai after the First World War. The cinema was built in 1953. Typical of the period is the lettering on the tall non-functional tower and the variety of decorative geometric patterning on different parts of the facade.

The Rediffusion Building on Clemenceau Avenue was also built by Palmer and Turner in 1948-9. Their MacDonald House for the Hongkong and Shanghai Bank in Orchard Road of the same year was the first tall building erected after the war in Singapore, rivalling the pre-war Cathay Building. Both still stand today. The Cathay Building has been refaced in green tiles while MacDonald House still has its brick exterior with stucco window frames and Chinese tiled roofs, and travertine cladding to the ground floor. The high quality of the detailing has lasted well. At the top of MacDonald House are flats for Hongkong Bank employees.

149

Further buildings by Palmer and Turner at this time were an office headquarters for Guthries in 1951-2 in Battery Road; and the Bank of China Building in Battery Road in 1953-4. This latter demonstrates the firm's ability to design in a variety of styles: Bank of China Building is in the tradition of the first American skyscrapers. The supervising architect was in fact an American. The firm had built many similar tall buildings in Shanghai before the War. The Bank is built on a solid outcrop of rock, rare in Singapore, and needed no deep foundations. The building was one of the highest of its time in the city. The Bank of China occupied a grand banking hall and the low offices behind the tower. The offices in the tower were let out to private companies. Although this was the first building to be centrally airconditioned in Singapore, to the modern eye the high ceilings are old fashioned. It was some years later that, to save space and energy, ceilings were lowered to eight feet. The finishings on the building are of high quality. The original bronze doors and windows are still in place, and the stone finish on the facade is in fact very high quality stucco, grooved to look like stones. The Mercantile Bank Building, demolished in 1984, was rendered in a similar way.

The post war period also saw the first Singaporean architects return from architectural school in Britain. Ng Keng Siang was among these returnees. One of his buildings in the commercial area still stands on the corner of Finlayson Green and Raffles Quay — the Asia Insurance Building. Ng Keng Siang was a wealthy man, and really did not need to practise at all, but the Asia Insurance Building demonstrates — at least externally — that he had talent for orchestrating a facade and creating a distinctive roof-line. Although it is now dwarfed by skyscrapers one can still catch glimpses from afar of its spiral topnot at the corner of the roof. He had made an inverse feature of the corner — setting it back from the bands which tie the building together. The horizontal fenestration is very successful, emphasized by sunshades above them, in a cream marblite finish which has worn well. In 1984, similar fenestration was built into the Neptune Orient Lines (NOL) Building in Alexandra Road, with the same satisfying effect. The main entrance to the Asian Insurance Building is blocked these days, so that the secondary side entrance has gained more importance than originally intended. Inside the door can be seen the plaques of the offices inside, all attached higgledy-piggledy to the walls, suggestive of a rabbit warren, a sight familiar in older office buildings in the established business quarters of cities throughout the world. The fact that Singapore now has so few such buildings gives the Asia Insurance Building a strong air of nostalgia, and one hopes it will continue to survive.

The 1950's was a time of discovery about new materials and new methods of making foundations. In the field of commercial buildings there was also experimentation going on. In the early plans of the decade for the layout of the commercial district along reclaimed Robinson Road and Shenton Way, it was reckoned that the maximum height of the buildings would be ten storeys for the ground would not support higher buildings. A short-lived attitude! New methods were used to dig down to solid rock for foundations below the surface. Underground rivers with sweet water were found, as was sandstone to support these buildings, despite digging techniques which must have been rudimentary. In the 1950's parcels of land in the commercial district were bought by contractors and

Bank of China Building, Battery Road.
Palmer and Turner, 1953–54

speculators for commercial development. It took so long to find out what could and could not be built, however, that after two years, many of the building permits were rescinded as the contractors had not built within the required time. By that time, the market had slumped, anyway. Looking back, it is fortunate that these buildings were not built, and that the new plans of 1960 could take shape unhindered.

The construction of shop houses continued in this period, although the style was very much simpler than in the decades before the war. The same width of 20 feet per shophouse was maintained, but construction was more often in concrete, rather than the original timbers. Now only the simplest of rectangular windows pierced the facade, and virtually no plaster decoration was applied to the stucco facade. The result is much less attractive than the earlier shophouses as without the ornamentation, the basic shape is so simple. Sadly, one sees many instances of 1950's adaptations of the earlier frontages. Many owners of houses in South Boat Quay, for example, were intent on modernizing their dwellings, extracting all the charming details.

In 1958 the Nanyang University (now the Nanyang Institute of Technology) was created in Jurong on a huge unoccupied site. A Chinese-inspired building was designed for the administration offices. A central pavilion with a Chinese roof is flanked by two wings of equal length, made of red brick. The pastiche effect of Chinese detailing on a box-like structure is more marked on a building of this length. The result is not as successful as the China Building for OCBC, or the Chinese Chamber of Commerce in Hill Street, both buildings of the same ilk.

When the PAP came to power in 1959, the housing and commercial situation in Singapore was dire. When they withdrew, the British left severe economic and un-

employment problems behind them. The Singapore Improvement Trust had not been able to keep pace with an overwhelming need for new public housing. Squatter areas and shanty towns were in a desperate state, with no amenities. Soon after Independence, Singapore applied for and received a grant from the United Nations to bring in planning experts to teach local government personnel how to plan for Singapore's future development, and to create an organization to implement it. A fundamental change towards strong central planning of the city was put into practice, and the process continues today. Its success is remarkable and owes much to the foresight and strength of mind of those who implemented it.

At the outset, emphasis was put on an integrated development programme of building public housing, while at the same time organizing industrial expansion and urban development in the central area. Triple and interlocking objectives were set out. The building of housing would create jobs for the workforce in large numbers in the construction industry. New industries also had to be encouraged as the entrepot trade on which Singapore had historically depended had ceased to provide sufficient scope for economic growth. Jurong Town Corporation (JTC) was created to cope with the development of industry, requiring a skilled workforce; with an area for pollutant heavy industry carefully located away from the main centres of population. JTC worked with the Housing and Development Board to provide housing close to the workplace. Gradually, JTC became responsible for many industrial sites scattered over the island. It pioneered flatted factories near suitable facilities for their particular needs; e.g. timber businesses near Sungei Kranji with good water facilities.

A special department was created to deal with the central area, designated the financial centre of Singapore. The Urban

*Nanyang University (Institute of
Technology), Jurong, 1958, (top)*

*Asia Insurance Building, Finlayson
Green. Ng Keng Siang, 1954,
(bottom)*

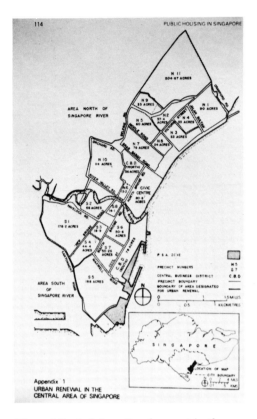

Plan of Central Area Development in the 1960's

Renewal Department evolved into the Urban Renewal Authority (URA) which undertook the sale of sites for redevelopment to private companies. The central area was divided into sections and numbered according to the priority of their development. The properties south of the river had S. numbers and the parcels of land north of the river had N. numbers. The first priority for development was given to areas on the fringes of the business district, such as Havelock Road, Outram Road, the Golden Mile, and Crawford Street. The intention was to move gradually toward the centre, once the population had been relocated. The first two numbered districts were areas of bad slum and squatter housing. However, blocks of flats were deliberately built in this area in order to keep the population in the centre of the city.

The principal responsibility of the HDB was to create new towns outside the central area. These surfaced in the form of towns such as Queenstown and Toa Payoh in the 1960's, Ang Mo Kio and Bedok in the 1970's, and Hougang and Tampines in the 1980's. The first blocks to be built provided the basic facilities with no frills. Later developments corresponded to the upgrading policy of the board, as the basic need for rehousing out of slum areas became less pressing. Some of their original flats have even been renovated and expanded by the HDB.

To create increased building land in the central district and to fulfill the proven requirements of recreational land for a happy population, a massive reclamation programme was started on the East Coast, creating the East Coast Parkway recreation area, with beaches and holiday bungalows, campsites and sports facilities. On the West Coast reclamation projects were also undertaken for recreation land, and for increased dock facilities in Jurong.

Other economic priorities were also selected. One was the need to attract foreign visitors. Creation of hotels and shopping facilities was encouraged in the Orchard Road area and by the 1980's many new hotels had been completed. New recreational facilities have been created to attract foreign tourists, such as the Japanese and Chinese Gardens, Jurong Bird Park, the Singapore Zoo and Sentosa Island.

The Bird Park and the Zoo were cleverly sited, the former in the middle of an industrial area, as an oasis of greenery and an interchanger for polluted air with regeneration from the trees. The Zoo is sited next to Pierce Reservoir, thus making use of conserved land for clean recreational facilities. Next door are many of the orchid nurseries and farms that

Flats, Queenstown. H.D.B. 1964, (top)   *Flats, Telok Blangah New Town. H.D.B. 1978, (bottom)*

provide markets and flower shops with their daily produce.

In a symposium on planning in Singapore given by the URA in April 1984 the original architects of the redevelopment of the island marvelled at how effective the programme had been and how close to the original master plan the island had developed. Prime Minister Lee Kuan Yew's government had the political power to ensure through legislation that the reforms would be carried out and that the implementing organizations such as the HDB and JTC would have the jurisdiction and the power to make the necessary changes. By 1984 some 75% of the population live in HDB flats, and by the turn of the century the plans are that 90% will live in public housing.

The other wonder, from the point of view of the Westerner, is that the HDB flats, looking rather drab and boring from the outside, really do seem to work socially. Residents' committees and community centres play an effective role in uniting the three races who live in them all mixed up together, as do wet markets and cinemas. Perhaps the key is in the fact that most flats are sold and that the people have pride of ownership and interest in keeping up their homes.

The significance of the HDB flats is in their quantity, as most of them could hardly be classed as innovative architecture, until the most recent efforts at varying the silhouettes and exteriors. It is in their social success that they are interesting. The sloped roofs of the flats at Potong Pasir, and the fortress-like quality of some flats near Serangoon Road mark them out as something different,

Rowell Court Flats, off Serangoon Road.
HDB 1983, (top)

Singapore Conference Hall, Shenton Way.
Design Partnership, 1968, (bottom)

and the residents will at least have something visual by which to identify them, rather than just a number and a Lorong. The ultimate aim is for the island to be ringed with new towns to spread the population away from the central districts. The outlying towns will be connected to the centre by the Mass Rapid Transit (MRT) system, which started construction in 1983. This is the last major objective of the overall Singapore plan.

Most of the energies in the 1960's went into planning rather than completion of new buildings; most of the early buildings from the URA sales of sites came to fruition only in the seventies. Besides the sites that the URA sanctioned for development, there were the private speculations, and the public buildings on reclaimed land. Among the latter, one of the first was the Singapore Conference Hall in Shenton Way. It was built to house trade union conferences, but was turned into a multi-purpose hall before the modernization of the Victoria Memorial Concert Hall and Theatre was completed. Produced by Design Partnership, it has weathered the intervening years very well. An unusual feature of the auditorium is the very steep bank of auditorium seats after a flat floor, designed to bring the delegates at the back closer to the podium and give a more immediate atmosphere to the meetings there.

One the great symbols of nationhood of the 1960's celebrating the emerging independent Singapore, was the National Theatre at the corner of Clemenceau and River Valley Road. The money for its construction was collection by public subscription and the building was given a revolutionary new design. The great cantilevered roof and the auditorium open to the sky signified the freedom and collectiveness of the nation. At the beginning of 1984, a new era in the development of the community was

*People's Park Complex,
Eu Tong Sen Street.
Design Partnership, 1970, (top)*

*Marco Polo Hotel, Tanglin
Road. Alfred Wong, 1962,
(bottom)*

Ming Court Hotel, Tanglin Road. Kumpulan Akitek, 1970, (top)

Modern Palladian Motif, Window, Cockpit Hotel, Penang Road, 1960, (bottom)

reached when the National Theatre was condemned on structural grounds and on the ground that it had outgrown its usefulness. It will be pulled down. Certainly it had become too hot for audiences now accustomed to air-conditioning, and traffic noise had not been effectively excluded, a disturbing distraction from the performances being held there. The National Theatre was built by Alfred Wong and Partners, one of the first of the post-war generation of architects to return to Singapore. He has built a number of noteworthy buildings in the city and elsewhere.

The National Library Building was completed next to the Museum in 1953 thus relieving pressure on the Museum for its ever expanding collection of books and microfilms. It has the mark of a 1950's building, being built of red brick with a flat roof and a projecting roof-line. It is in the same generation of buildings as the Hongkong and Shanghai Bank's MacDonald House in Orchard Road.

In the area of public building, mention must be made of the second Singapore Airport at Paya Lebar, which was built further out of town than the first Kallang Airport. Kallang Airport was transformed to house the People's Association, and the airfield was covered by the National Stadium designed by Kenzo Tange in the 1960's.

In the private sector the first evidence of the new commercialization of Orchard Road was the twenty storey high Cockpit Hotel in Penang Road. It is chiefly remarkable for its Venetian style windows, a transplant from an earlier era of architecture. The Marco Polo Hotel, originally called Hotel Malaysia, was built in Tanglin Road in the 1960's by Alfred Wong. It had a roof top restaurant in the early days. It was later extended by another wing which has been well integrated into the earlier curved design. The Ming Court Hotel, which opened in 1970,

was one of the first to be built in Orchard Road itself. Its dominant roofs have been called oriental, but the reference is not specific. The grouping of the building components is very satisfactory and Kumpulan Akitek have made a success of the building.

The People's Park Complex, finished in October 1970, scored several firsts in Singapore. Its name as well as the block of flats is the closest to Le Corbusier's ideal of high-rise living, as expressed in his Marseilles Habitation, both in concept and in form. A dominant roofscape is typical, but Design Partnership architects added the impressive verticals which dominate the visual impact of the block. A variety of apartment sizes is accommodated here, and access to them is independent of the shopping centre below. The shopping centre incorporates the first "city room" or atrium in Singapore, a concept that was pioneered by several Japanese architects in the 1960's.

As has been said, the 1960's were devoted to defining the sites, choosing the priorities among types of buildings that could be built: offices, hotels, shopping centres, private flats — and putting into motion the machinery that would bring these plans to fruition. The results of the new planning and organization undertaken by the United Nations and Singapore teams began to bear fruit in the 1970's.

National Stadium, Kallang, Kenzo Tange, 1973, (top)

National Theatre, Clemenceau Avenue, Alfred Wong and Partners, 1963, (bottom)

'The Esplanade' by A.L. Watson, 1905–10,
oil on canvas, (top)

View from Esplanade, 1985,
(bottom)

A VIEW OF TODAY
1970 — 1985

The physical transformation of Singapore since 1973 is one of the wonders of the architectural and planning world. At a seminar to mark the 10th Anniversary of the Urban Redevelopment Authority, Professor E Lorange, the Norwegian town planner who in 1958 worked on a plan for redeveloping the centre of Singapore, was astonished to see the fruits of his efforts so comprehensively realized. Prime Minister Lee Kuan Yew's government has had both the power and the will to haul Singapore out of the quagmire of stagnation in the fifties and to remake it into one of the centres of efficiency and progress in a region that has been beset by development problems. For the last 20 years architects firms have mushroomed — a recent list counted over 150 in this small island. The pressure of getting buildings built has meant vast expansion of the construction industry, for local firms as well as the foreign firms of the region — especially from Japan and South Korea. Nevertheless, while it may seem churlish to criticize such momentous achievement, pressure to design and build fast, with many projects on the drawing board at one time, has meant that many of the design solutions have not been as well considered as they might have been in a less frenetic period.

While there is much good modern design in Singapore, it is the exception rather than the rule. To the foreign eye, Singapore's modern look is insufficiently distinguishable from the cities in the West. We believe that 1984 is seeing a move towards a definition of Singapore's identity in physical terms accompanying celebrations of 25 years of nationhood. At 25 years the new adult is passing into the phase of more experience and greater maturity, with an urge to round his own immediate experience into a larger whole. For example, maturity implies a proper appreciation of the importance of the past in one's present make up. The modernization of Singapore has been accomplished with a laudable but only very limited effort at preserving buildings of historic interest or significance. The monuments that have been preserved under the Preservation of the Monuments Board 1973 are largely religious — temples of two religions, churches and mosques of two more. The mature phase of conservation and adaptation involves contexts as well as monuments, and much of Singapore's older architecture is on a very small scale compared to modern buildings: a small mosque building (such as the Abdul Gaffoor) loses its significance unless it is in contact with the houses around it. So much has been built as high rise, in offices, hotels or flats, that Singapore may soon be characterized by the aerial rather than the ground view.

A selection of buildings commissioned by the government or by the town councils will give a microcosmic view of modern architecture in Singapore as a whole. These include several high rise blocks, courts, town halls, and the new Changi Airport. It is necessarily a snapshot view: the story of modern buildings in Singapore deserves a book of its own. Indeed, some very exciting buildings are now emerging, and will continue to emerge, as new building techniques are developed and perfected.

First, one feature of Singapore's modern architecture has been the role played by foreign architects, and their influence on the local profession. World famous architects such as I.M. Pei, Kenzo Tange and John Portman have put their name to several buildings. I.M. Pei designed the OCBC Centre (1976), Raffles City (1985), and the Gateway Project (1986) in Beach Road. Kenzo Tange was responsible for the National Stadium Complex, Nanyang Institute of Technology's new buildings and the OUB Building in Raffles Place. Tange will link this building into the MRT station in Raffles Place. John Portman first designed the Pavilion International Hotel and more recently has designed the three hotels in Marina Square.

I.M.Pei is world renowned for formalistic buildings of exciting character. The OCBC Centre has curved twin cores with office space suspended on huge transverse girders between them. The construction of the building was a challenge for the industry and has contributed to Singapore's short list of distinguished buildings. It's prominent position behind the Singapore River means that it has become a well-known landmark. The twin cores reflect the image that OCBC wishes to project to the public — "Solid as a Rock" — reflected in the sturdiness of dual supports rather than the more usual single core. Further, the three sets of neat rectangular windows suggest a connection with modern technology — indeed the suggestion has rooted itself in the public's mind, as it is often referred to as the "calculator building".

The supervising architects, BEP Architects, next won the commission for the Telecoms headquarters in Exeter Road. Although the external aspect of this building is clean and less detailed than OCBC (apart from the communications paraphernalia bristling on the roof), the unmistakable reference is to a twin core building with office space projecting forward from the core, a distinct quotation from the OCBC Centre.

John Portman has given Singapore a type of hotel designed especially for the hot weather and verdant foliage. His balconied floors overlooking a central open space which rises from floor to ceiling drip with vines and bougainvillea flower in boxes outside the windows, softening the geometricality of the exterior — always a problem in hotel design. The first hotel he built here was the Pavilion Intercontinental: the play of contrasting shapes in the public areas, the movement of water, give a theatricality to the interior space that makes being there an experience. In his Marina Square, the shapes of his hotels are more sculptural, and not particularly high rise.

Kenzo Tange has made his foreign reputation as much in the field of town planning as in architecture. He advised on the layout of the Kallang Sports Complex, built on the former aerodrome, and has been commissioned to build a mini-town on the hilly terrain of the Nanyang Institute of Technology site. Tange specializes in bridging valleys, and creating building spines on ridges. Nanyang is an ideal site to display this exciting building concept.

The role of foreign architects is carefully controlled in Singapore to ensure that the local profession will enjoy a degree of protection. The foreigners' presence has been beneficial in introducing new types of designs and building methods, and has extended and modernized the horizons of the Singapore archi-

Comcentre (Telecoms), Exeter Road. BEP Architects, 1978, (top)

Pavilion Intercontinental, Cuscaden Road. J. Portman, 1983, (bottom)

tecture and building industry. A description of a very small selection of high and low rise government buildings will illustrate the variety of design solutions, the freedom to open projects to competition from the private sector, and the positive reflection on the government's architecture that these buildings demonstrate.

The striking Central Provident Fund (CPF) Building, constructed by the Public Works Department and the first of two high rise buildings to be selected, stands in Robinson Road, next door to the Development Bank of Singapore (DBS) Building, with which it harmonizes. Both buildings are set on a podium — a planning stipulation for all buildings along Shenton Way so that buildings further removed from the sea may keep a view. The CPF Building was finished in 1977. The two basement floors house The Board of Commissioners of Currency and the first and second levels house the CPF. The treatment of these two levels in white tiles with slit windows piercing both floors gives a solid base to the floating three levels of car parking above, and the dark dignified 40 storey tower rising out of it. The tower block consists of four sections suspended from a central service core. The sections of the tower are separated from each other at the 17th, 27th and 30th floors — at these levels are the mechanical plant and fire fighting equipment.

Ventilators also appear at these junctures — they are made a feature at the base, seeming to support the whole structure and tying together the vertical aluminium strips which run the whole length of the building. The vertical members further stiffen the light weight curtain wall. The core runs up the centre of the building and pushes out through the top. The whole hangs together as a well

CPF Building, Robinson Road. Public Works Department, 1977

arranged sober unit, and is one of the most elegant of the tall downtown buildings.

The other high rise building constructed for the government is the Public Utilities Board (PUB) Building, the result of a competition held in 1971. The building accommodates several departments of the Board which had outgrown the existing office space in City Hall. The architects, Tan Puay Huat and Ong Chin Bee of Group 2 Architects designed an H-shaped plan. The two wings of unequal height are linked on the ground and first two floors by a wider transverse area and further up by the lift shaft and the access to each floor. The building rises 17 storeys and has a swimming pool on the roof. It also houses an auditorium besides the offices for the PUB and outside companies. Externally, the two long facades graduate irregularly in width and length by chamfered steps. These chamfers soften the corners of the building. At the ends the length is emphasized and the various design elements of the facade are tied together visually by vertical projections housing the staircase. This building is remarkable in the fact that the original design was executed virtually without later alteration on a rather surprising site — behind the hotels in Orchard Road, and ultimately to be surrounded by an MRT station, shopping complexes and blocks of flats. The PUB and Telecoms buildings really belong downtown. However, they stand out even more in their mid-town isolation.

The Urban Redevelopment Authority (URA) has been active since 1974 overseeing the planning and visual aspect of the central area of Singapore. They have also been instrumental in preserving and readapting some old buildings with a view to attracting tourists. One such example is the Singapore Handicraft Centre in Tanglin Road between two large hotels, and near several shopping centres. A row

Singapore Handicraft Centre, Tanglin Road. 1978, (above)

PUB Building, Somerset Road. Group 2 Architects, 1973, (opposite)

of old terraced houses in the English Tudor half-timbered style, have been adapted to form offices for the Singapore Tourist Promotion Board and next door, built alongside and behind, are a stepped series of arcaded blocks housing shops selling and demonstrating handicrafts of the South East Asian region. Above are two storeys of accommodation. The multi levels give interest to the arcades and as the courtyards lead into each other there are no back views to spoil the aura of peacefulness and greenery. There is adequate shade, variety of visual interest, and successful interpenetration of space.

Soon after the Jurong Town Corporation (JTC) was set up in 1969 it was decided to hold a competition to select the best design for a Town Hall to house the administration. The winning design, by Raymond Woo, is most interesting. Situated on a small hill, it has an H ground plan somewhat similar to the PUB Building. The two blocks lie parallel to each other and are of unequal length. In the centre is a skylight, while suspended over the central area on one half of the building is a large conference room. The top two floors are cantilevered outwards on the exterior of the building as well as in the lightwell. Part of the building is used by the JTC and the rest is let out to private firms. There is a conference hall on the ground floor as well as two committee rooms, a restaurant and a lecture theatrette for 100 people. The construction on columns gives maximum freedom.

Two stipulations of the brief determinded the external aspect of the building. One was that it had to be distinctive and symbolic; and the other was that it had to have commanding views of the countryside. The building seems to float on its hillock above the trees, with its periscope clock tower giving the whole a rather animate aspect. The building was started in 1976 and completed in three years.

In the Subordinate Courts in Havelock Road, Kumpulan Akitek, a private architectural firm, devised an ingenious building from a challenging brief, at the same time creating an interesting and integrated

Jurong Town Hall, Jurong, Raymond Woo, 1970, (top)

Interior, Jurong Town Hall, Jurong, Raymond Woo, 1970, (bottom)

Subordinate Courts, Havelock Road, Kumpulan Akitek, 1974, (opposite)

external visual whole.

The building spins off in eight directions from a central core, containing four massive columns. These support a conference room floor which covers the central open space. The open metal space frame at the top of the atrium gives a lightness to the atrium which counterbalances the massiveness of the columns.

The building comprises ten levels, many of which are confined to half floors and mezzanines. Twenty-six courts are housed in the four wings on the lower levels, with a large courtroom on the lower central floor. The building also houses a registry library, solicitors bar room, judges chambers, witness rooms and a canteen. Forty-four prisoner cells are located in the basement. Two entrances serve the prisoners. A multi-level exclusive traffic system divides areas used by the magistrates, judges, prisoners and the public. Four service cores contain six lift shafts, stairways and stores. Marble facing in the public areas gives dignity to the whole and sound proof material clads the courtrooms. The exterior is finished with white and grey exposed aggregate. The courts function efficiently at all levels, the judiciary process is centralized and the visual impact of the court house is striking.

The last two buildings to be mentioned demonstrate the government's constant consideration of pollution levels and of designing with physical terrain in mind.

The first is the National University of Singapore, built along and behind Kent Ridge, on a spectacular site between Ayer Rajah Road and Pasir Panjang Road, and bounded along one side by Clementi Road.

The development of University buildings at Kent Ridge gathered together in one place a formerly scattered group of University faculties. A master plan for the site was drawn up in 1969-71 by a Dutch firm OD 205 under the leadership of architect Joshua van Embden. The four principal aims of his brief were the preservation of the basic character of the site, integrity of function, ease of communication, and flexibility of usage. The projections were for a maximum student population of 8,000. Phase One, started in November 1973 and completed in 1977, provided accommodation for the Faculty of Engineering and engineering workshops, the Faculty of Architecture & Building, the Department of Physics & Mathematics, the Computer Centre, the Students Centre, the Central Administration, the School of Accountancy & Business Administration, and the Central Library. In the plans all buildings provide for future expansion.

The buildings were designed to stand on either side of the Ridge, following the undulating contours of the land. The landscape dictated a curved ground plan. No building is over five storeys high and most buildings are between three and five floors.

A uniform grid was devised for each structure and most have cantilevered balconies. The large span buildings were designed to house laboratories and workshops. The third type of building has a non-uniform structural grid. These house such facilities as lecture rooms, dining halls and the sports stadium.

The plan is very spacious, with sweeping green swards, their curves often accentuated by walkways or roads, well shaded by trees. The campus is a delight to move through. The architects separated pedestrian traffic from motor traffic along the main spines of academic buildings. Chains of buildings are linked together by double storeyed walkways, roofed to give protection from the sun and rain. These rise and fall with the landscape, their form disciplined with steps and handrails.

In most of the academic buildings the external wall is set back with a screen-and-grid balcony effect providing shade and giving formal overall patterning to the exteriors. The administration block is physically differentiated by the greater severity of its banded exterior. Stair wells are used as an architectural feature, punctuating

the division of one block from another. They stand taller than the main body of the buildings. Variety is further provided through the use of flat and pitched roofs. Visually the whole is very pleasing and successful.

Materials for external finishes have been carefully chosen to weather well. Many steps and walkways are brick, with a rusty glow; coloured tiles and bright handrails vary the more sober white and tiled exterior walls. Lecture halls are finished in wood for acoustic reasons. The human scale is well maintained throughout, the landscape provides visual variety and a healthy green environment. In the design of the buildings the architects have taken the hot climate into consideration, both actually and visually, in breaking up surfaces, giving play to light and shade, and conveying a sense of the delicate character of tropical flora.

At the other end of the island, built completely on reclaimed land, with its noise and air polluting activities far away from the residential estates, lies Changi Airport. It has been acclaimed by numerous travellers as one of the most beautiful and efficient airports. From an architectural and planning point of view, it would certainly compete effectively as one of the best in the world, and deserves an assessment here.

It was completed in early 1981. After some study the airport planners had decided to use tried and true concepts and equipment for their airport. They selected Schiphol Airport in Amsterdam as their standard of judgment and asked Dutch experts for assistance in such matters as traffic forecasting and peak hour passenger movement. The PWD architects plan to have three and possibly four terminals, if and when the need arises. The second is planned to open in 1985, the third if necessary, in 1992. What the planners learned from Amsterdam is that the simplest possible way of transferring

Central Administration, National University
of Singapore, Kent Ridge. OD 205, 1977,
(top)

National University of Singapore, general
view following contour of the hill,
(bottom)

Control Tower, Changi Airport. PWD, 1981

passengers between planes and ground transportation is the most efficient. To that end they designed a Passenger Terminal Building (PTB) in the shape of an H — the body of which houses the arrival and departure facilities, lounges, restaurants and administrative offices, and the wings of which house boarding lounges leading to parking bays for the aircraft. The building is five storeys high, of which three serve the public. Bus departures and arrivals are at basement level, arrivals on the ground floor, departures on the second floor, with restaurants on a mezzanine level above. The third floor has lounges and restaurants. Public access from one floor to another is by moving travellators and ramps, and circulation works well.

Energy conservation was a major consideration in the design. Glassed-in areas were reduced to a minimum. Bay windows were designed for the first and second floors — behind which opens up the high ceilinged departure hall. The third floor has a minimum of windows. The roof is composed of folded segments to reflect the bay windows. The variety of outline given to the roof, slightly raised in the centre, relieves the monotony of the great length of the facade. The whole building is supported on pillars which give a modular effect, and provide great flexibility in the disposition of interior facilities. The large spaces are broken up inside, by the two lifts and stairways, running vertically through the PTB.

The interior effects were achieved by two designers, Indeco and Bent Severin & Associates. In accordance with the wishes of the PWD, they kept the interior simple and uncluttered, and introduced to the public the garden city character of Singapore. Earth tones dominate as they harmonize with plants and water, an integral part of the interior design. Two spectacular curtain fountains send water through the three levels of the PTB down

Interior, Changi Airport. Indeco, 1981

mylar cords creating a bead effect. As it hits the base pool, the water spouts up into a dome shaped spray. The fountain — like the lift shafts — unites the building vertically. Other fountains are strategically placed for maximum impact. Fountains in the arrival hall, audible and visible as the passenger descends the escalator to the immigration desks, sooth tired nerves and soften the massiveness of the architecture. In the departure lounge area two fountains designed like sheets of water mark the seating area, carpeted as in a hotel lobby, for passengers waiting for a flight or enduring a delay. The reminder that Singapore is an island republic is further stated in the two large aquaria in the arrival hall. A plant nursery, covering 15 hectares of airport land ensures that the plants, both for the outside and — especially orchids — for the interior displays, are always fresh.

The ceilings of the very large interior spaces were chosen on the criteria of good acoustic rating, requiring minimal maintenance, and being able to incorporate ventilation ducts, air-conditioning outlets and light fixtures. Aluminium baffles met these stipulations and relieve the monotony of the large area they cover.

Materials for the interior underwent rigorous tests for their acoustic properties and were chosen for their good performance. Certainly for its size, Changi Airport is a surprisingly quiet building.

The control tower that is the landmark in the approach to the airport was an interesting feat of engineering. The sixteen-sided three-tiered cabin was constructed on the ground and raised up the cylindrical shaft. The method of lifting, by four jacks and 32 lifting bars was very laborious. Six metres a day was achieved, taking two weeks in total.

In which direction, then, will Singapore be going in the future? We believe that it will remain, as it always has been, architecturally dominated by Western influences. As the building boom shows signs of slackening, more thought will be concentrated on good architecture, with quality materials and finer proportions. Kenzo Tange, the designer of the elegant OUB Building, now rising in Raffles Place, and master planner extraordinaire, feels there is still scope in Marina South for a group of spectacular tall buildings relating to each other. He has plans for about 40 for Singapore, and no doubt so do others. Architects and government officials are on the whole still sadly unsentimental about old architecture, most of which is very small scale, and which, to present a cohesive entity

Marina Square, Nicoll Highway. J. Portman, 1985, (top). Model (bottom)

and proper context, would need to be preserved on a large scale, at least five square city blocks. There is some evidence that thoughts are turning to preservation and adaptive reuse. There were several seminars in 1984 on the subject and several houses in Emerald Hill, Saunders Road, and River Valley Road have been renovated to their original attractive designs. However, until the government is willing to underwrite the financial loss of real estate returns incurred in preserving a large area which might otherwise be redeveloped, there is not much hope that any significant progress will be made in this area. However, historical bodies do exist, and the school history curriculum has recently been revised to incorporate more awareness of Singapore's colourful past.

One must admire the progress made by the government since 1960 in revamping the face of Singapore in all aspects of life. The future will hold a great challenge for the island nation, as it sits poised on a watershed — economically, socially, architecturally. There are many advantages here — a peaceful multi-racial society, prosperity, cleanliness, good health, and growing cultural awareness. Progress will reflect itself in all these areas, as well as in buildings old and new in the future. Since Raffles arrived, Singapore has been a nursery of enterprise, a home for talented people, willing to make the effort to succeed; and in making that effort, willing to constantly update their environment to meet their economic and social needs. As has been mentioned, in 1929, an American visitor to Singapore commented on the amazing changes in the look of Singapore over the previous decade. In 1990, 2000 and onwards, it seems highly likely that on returning to Singapore, each visitor will be similarly amazed at the country's willingness and ability to change and adapt.

Selected Bibliography

Archer, Mildred and Bastin, John. *The Raffles Drawings,* 1968.

Archives and Oral History Department. *Singapore Retrospect Through Postcards, 1900-1930,* Singapore, 1982.

Archives and Oral History Department. *Chinatown,* Singapore, 1983.

Boyd, A. *Chinese Architecture and Town Planning,* London, 1962.

Buckley, C.B. *An Anecdotal History of Old Times in Singapore, 1819-1867,* Singapore, 1902, reprinted, Kuala Lumpur, 1965.

Comber, Leon. *Chinese Temples in Singapore,* Singapore 1958.

Davis, D. *Old Singapore,* Singapore, 1954.

Gan Eng Oon, Ed. *Rumah, Contemporary Architecture of Singapore,* Singapore, 1981.

Hall-Jones, John. *The Thomson Paintings,* Singapore 1983.

Hall-Jones, J. and Hooi. C. *An Early Surveyor in Singapore,* Singapore, 1979.

Hancock, T.H.H. and Gibson-Hill, C.A. *Architecture in Singapore,* Singapore 1954.

King, A.D. *Colonial Urban Development,* London, 1976.

Lee Kip Lin. *Telok Ayer Market,* Singapore, 1983.

Lee Kip Lin. *Emerald Hill Road,* Singapore, 1984.

Lip, Evelyn. *Chinese Temple Architecture in Singapore,* Singapore, 1963.

Lip, Evelyn. *Chinese Temples and Deities,* Singapore, 1953.

Journal of The Malaysian Branch of The Royal Asiatic Society. *Singapore-150 Years,* Singapore, 1982.

Makepeace, W.E., Braddell, R.St. and Brooke, G.S. Eds. *One Hundred Years of Singapore,* Vols. 1 and 2, London, 1921.

Mialaret, J.P. *Hinduism in Singapore,* Singapore, 1958.

Moore, Donald and Joanna. *The First Hundred and Fifty Years of Singapore,* Singapore, 1959.

Morris, Jan, Winchester, Simon. *Stones of Empire,* Oxford, 1983.

Nilsson, Sten. *European Architecture in India, 1750-1850,* London, 1968.

National Museum. *Singapore Rediscovered,* Singapore, 1983.

Ramachandra, S. *Singapore Landmarks, Past and Present,* Singapore, 1960.

Sharp, Ilsa. *There is Only One Raffles,* Singapore, 1982.

Siddique, Sharon, Shotam, Nirmala, Puru. *Singapore's Little India, Past, Present and Future,* Singapore, 1982.

Singapore Coordinating Committee (text, M. Gretchen). *Pastel Portraits, Singapore's Architectural Heritage,* Singapore, 1984.

Song Ong Siang. *One Hundred Years History of the Chinese in Singapore,* London, 1923, reprinted, Singapore, 1967, 1985.

Turnbull, C.M. *A History of Singapore, 1819-1975,* Kuala Lumpur, 1977.

Tyers, R. *Singapore Then and Now,* Vols. 1 and 2, Singapore, 1976.

Watson, W.I., *Swan and Maclaren, A Historical Profile,* 1885-1979.

Periodicals

Housing and Development Board. *Annual Report, 1983.*

Journal of the Federation of Malaya Society of Architects,
        Vol. 1-2. 1951-2
        Vol. 3-4. 1953-4
        Vol. 2   1957-9

Lim, William, "Public Housing and Community Development". *MIMAR,* No. 7, 1983.

Keys, Peter. "Straits Chinese Terrace Houses in Singapore.", *Orientations,* June, 1983.

Planews, Journal of the Singapore Institute of Planners.
        Vol. 3, No. 1, 1973.
        Vol. 4, No. 1, 1973.
        Vol. 8, No. 1, 1981.

Straits Times Annuals, 1970-1983

Index